MY LIFE AND THE BEAUTIFUL MUSIC

MY LIFE AND THE BEAUTIFUL MUSIC

Jon Hotten

JONATHAN CAPE
LONDON

1 3 5 7 9 10 8 6 4 2

Jonathan Cape, an imprint of Vintage,
20 Vauxhall Bridge Road,
London SW1V 2SA

Jonathan Cape is part of the Penguin Random House
group of companies whose addresses can be found at
global.penguinrandomhouse.com.

Copyright © Jon Hotten 2015

Jon Hotten has asserted his right to be identified as
the author of this Work in accordance with the Copyright,
Designs and Patents Act 1988

First published by Jonathan Cape in 2015

www.vintage-books.co.uk

A CIP catalogue record for this book is available
from the British Library

ISBN 9780224077835

Penguin Random House is committed to a sustainable future
for our business, our readers and our planet. This book is made
from Forest Stewardship Council® certified paper.

Typeset in Dante MT Std by Palimpsest Book Production Limited,
Falkirk, Stirlingshire

Printed and bound in Great Britain by
Clays Ltd, St Ives PLC

To those who were there

LA forces you to become the person you really are.

Bret Easton Ellis

ACQUIRED SITUATIONAL NARCISSISM
1988

1. *Unicorn*

The first line of the book I bought at the airport said 'People are afraid to merge on freeways in Los Angeles', and then, and for a long time afterwards, it didn't occur to me that it might not be literal, or even true, because the people on the freeways that I saw drove in long, calm lines, perfectly beautiful in their gleaming cars, all headed at similar speed in similar directions.

So – America again, the cab on the 405 from LAX towards West Hollywood, the hills looming darkly ahead, Mulholland snaking through them, the canyons and the valley beyond, scenes that had over time become familiar to me but that had also retained that sense of alien otherness that made them evocative and exciting. A lot of the writers on the magazine affected a jaded, been-there, done-that attitude to Los Angeles and their many assignments there, said that they preferred New York or Berlin or Tokyo, but LA and its dream landscape had always done it for me. No one was merging as the cab passed Wilshire before turning off on to Sunset, the street lights on now as we passed the Roxy and the Rainbow and Gazzarri's and rock 'n' roll Ralph's, and the St James Club, and then a giant billboard with a picture of David Lee Roth climbing a vast rock face, the cab driver reaching over to turn up the radio as the DJ said he was about to play something by Night Ranger.

As he passed the Chateau Marmont I pulled the printed itinerary from out of my book where it was marking my page to check the hotel again. It would be one of four, it always was, for the writers and photographers travelling on record-company tabs: the Hyatt on Sunset, otherwise known as the Riot House, where the sign behind the desk at reception said 'Be nice to this customer, they might have just sold a million records'; the Hollywood Roosevelt, the faded deco glamour of which I had discovered one languid, endless afternoon by the pool drinking White Russians; the Mondrian, which someone from EMI records had told me recently was part-owned by David Coverdale of Whitesnake; and the Sunset Marquis, which wasn't on Sunset at all, but hidden away on Alto Loma Road, a hotel that described itself as 'a serene garden oasis', but that Hunter S. Thompson used to call 'the Loser's Hilton'. None were as famous as the Marmont, but the PRs had learned not to put any writers there because all of the stories they filed ended up being about the hotel rather than the band they were supposed to be writing about, how they broke into the bungalow where John Belushi OD-ed or saw the attic where Howard Hughes spied on girls through binoculars or how they took a photo like the one on the cover of a Gram Parsons album. Everyone thought that everything they were writing was being written for the first time, or at least better than it was before, when in fact they were just repeating themselves endlessly, again and again.

This was the fourth time I'd been over in four weeks and the trips were already merging, compressed by memory into one long, soft-focus month in which I conducted numerous interviews, saw numerous gigs and attended a three-day party at a house on a rocky outcrop just above the Rainbow Bar and Grill that a girl by the pool whispered to me used to belong to James Cagney but that now, more prosaically, was owned by the manager of Iron Maiden (later the same girl, glazed and drunk, got into a car and drove it down the hill at high speed, the brake lights pulsing on and off at each bend).

Waiting for me behind the desk at the Hyatt with my room key was a white envelope containing four or five fifty-dollar bills – per diems for the first part of the trip – and a note telling me that my name was on a guest list for a show at the Roxy that night. I pushed the notes into my pocket and walked into the bar to see if the free buffet was out yet. It wasn't. I dropped my bag, took the lift up to the rooftop pool and sat in the corner with a foot on the rail to read some more of the book, the evening traffic backing up on Sunset below.

★

When I was twenty years old and not quite out of college, I began writing for the magazine. I was studying journalism and part of the syllabus was a work placement. It was called *Kerrang!* (an onomatopoeia describing the sound of a highly amplified guitar) and its strapline was 'the Bible of Heavy Metal'. For me, it was. I owned every issue. Just the thought of calling the number, which I had memorised, provoked days of fear but when I got through, all they said was, 'How long do you want to come for?'

'Er, a week?'

'Okay then.'

A month after that I was in Hollywood, interviewing a hair band about living their dream. I had written some sample reviews and one thing had led to another. The writers didn't have contracts or agreements or anything beyond their name on the contributors list at the front of the magazine and 10p per word printed, paid by cheque once every fortnight. It was okay, because after a while I barely needed any money of my own. Someone else was always paying the bill: lunch, dinner, hotel, flights, cabs, drinks, entertainment. Free albums arrived in the post every day, free admission to gigs every night, then dinner, then a party . . . Once a month, a guy in dark glasses called Steve came around to the office and bought any records that we didn't want for cash and sold them at his shop off Leicester Square with the little 'For Promotional Use Only: Not For Resale' stickers still on them. Huge rolls of notes changed hands – Steve's entire supply came from the music mags. Any record-company lunch ended with the stock cupboard open and the offer of armfuls' more stuff, bound for Steve's shop. This was the deal, this was how it worked, and it was the perfect moment to live that way, in what would be the last great era of record-company profits, when all they had to do was put record-shaped things into the stores for them to sell in their millions. To promote the records they sent bands out on endless tours – years at a time, sometimes – and made videos for MTV and employed armies of radio pluggers to get them on the radio and hundreds of PRs to get them on to the covers of magazines. In Britain, there was only one magazine about heavy metal, and so we had every major record company in Europe and America lining up at the door, with their money and their bands and their promises and their gifts. The magazine carried ten feature stories a week, each a treasured slot to be competed for by PRs and publicists who were in turn driven on by label bosses and band managers that had invested their money and their careers in making a small percentage of these groups globally successful. Then there was us, the writers, ciphers with our strange kind of power over them all. Almost every band in the magazine was American and if they weren't they spent most of their time there, in the land of MTV and endless rock radio stations, a place where selling 500,000 records was simply a qualified success. The writers went from story to story, orbiting these satellites (in my first year at *Kerrang!* I spent almost three months there on the fabled I-Visa, that allowed the bearer in and out whenever they chose).

Throughout all of this I'd lived with a suspicion I had that I was an outsider, an observer rather than a participant, distinguished by the fact that I wore my hair short, dressed differently, didn't take drugs, barely drank, and as a result I often felt fearful and insecure, which lent my writing an iconoclastic streak that, when it worked, gave the magazine an edge that its editor, Geoff, liked to exploit, sometimes giving me assignments or reviews that he knew would result in provocative pieces that enraged their subjects, which they did – once a cardboard coffin with my name on it was delivered to reception; the manager of a band called Cinderella threatened to shove 50,000 copies of their new album 'up my ass'; a member of Mötley Crüe came looking for me with a baseball bat, and so on. I revelled in the infamy, and it made no difference anyway, because the records that I and the others wrote about stayed in the Billboard charts for months and then years, regardless of our opinions of them.

Yet what we didn't write was more important in sustaining it all. I didn't write about the drummer who shot speedballs with the girlfriend of his band's infinitely more famous singer, watched her OD and then had sex with her while she was unconscious on his kitchen floor; or about the singer who slept with the older wife of another rock star, a woman who had been pursuing him hungrily and whom he had been avoiding equally assiduously until he became so drunk that he could no longer recognise her (he told me later, his face drawn and white, that when he woke the next morning with her head on his shoulder he'd 'wished he could have gnawed his own arm off' rather than disturb her as he left); about the ageing guitarist I found sitting in a bathroom stall at the Long Beach Arena holding his wig in both hands and crying; the singer seriously contemplating a sex change (he later went ahead); the rock star who called his pregnant wife a 'germophobe' because she'd asked him to stop sharing needles and then having sex with her; the bass player who was, unbeknown to him, raising one of his bandmates' children as his own. I didn't write about any of that, ever, even though it went on right in front of me.

★

Later, I walked down to the Roxy, passing back under the David Lee Roth billboard, the ghost-whine of the aircraft engines still singing in my ears. It was a cool, bright night. I had to shout my name at the girl on the door – inside it was dark and airless, a band were already on and making the standard noises in front of an uninterested audience that included three other writers from the magazine, all in town on different assignments, and also Taime Downe, who ran a club called the Cathouse and sang in a band named Faster Pussycat, Rick Rubin, producer of the Beastie Boys and owner of Def American Recordings, and David Lee Roth, no longer halfway up a cliff face but standing at the back of the Roxy with his manager Pete Angelus; also present were Arlette Vereeke, a powerful PR for Roth, and a new band from the Strip who'd just signed to Geffen called Guns N' Roses, and Tom Zutaut, the A&R man who'd signed them; Riki Rachtman, who co-owned the Cathouse and another club called the Bordello which ran on Thursday nights, and Janine Lindemulder, who'd just been on the cover of *Penthouse*, and Marq Torien of the BulletBoys, and then a girl who looked like Demi Moore, and a guy who looked like River Phoenix – he coolly lit a cigarette and whispered in his girfriend's ear as the support band, who were called the Four Horsemen even though, inexplicably, there were five of them, finished their set and trooped off, and the Black Crowes, signed by Rick Rubin and managed by Pete Angelus, came on. They were young but they sounded old, and soon they and everyone in the room became caught up in what was happening, which was a giddy, escalating high in which the band fed the crowd and the crowd fed the band, each convincing the other that they were present at something special, and the band *were* good, but not that good, yet that wasn't how they would appear when tonight was written about: by the time everyone had finished telling each other that we were here seeing something that the world was yet to see, that is exactly what they would become.

The party afterwards was at a big white Spanish-style house up in the hills that was being rented by someone like Pete Angelus or Rick Rubin or Def American Recordings (it depended who you spoke to) from a movie producer or a music-biz lawyer or a big-time dope dealer who was lying low in Cabo – three people said three different things – and interior designers had been hired to turn the downstairs rooms and the pool area into some kind of Bedouin tent with Arabian carpets on the stone floors and patterned drapes hanging from the ceilings. People were lying on giant scatter cushions and smoking hookah pipes. Waitresses were dressed as belly dancers. Scorpions crawled around in fish tanks filled with sand. On one of the garden's lower tiers, a skittish white horse with a horn strapped to its head to make it look like a unicorn – it actually did – was being calmed by its handler, a lithe blonde girl in jodhpurs and black boots. I was checking out one of the belly-dancer waitresses, discreetly I felt, when a voice in my ear said, 'Busted . . .' and I turned around and saw Iris, this girl I knew from New York. She worked for a little record label in Manhattan and we'd met when I went over to interview one of her bands. The singer got a throat infection and couldn't speak, and Iris and me ended up together for two weeks while we waited for the singer's voice to come back. I learned all about her life. She was dating a drummer in a speed metal band that she was trying to manage in her spare time, using the few contacts she'd been able to make. Her record company had put me up in a once-grand, now decaying hotel called the Gramercy Park, where I had a huge, shabby suite stuffed with ageing furniture and far too near to an echoing, depthless lift shaft that rattled throughout the night. I'd lie there and listen to it moving up and down, the television tuned to a local channel that screened episodes of old cop shows, the sound low, the pictures casting shadows on the walls. I'd just drifted off to sleep one night when someone started banging on the door. It was Iris, wearing a long coat over her pyjamas. 'Fate has thrown us together,' she said as she took off the coat and got into bed. This was the first time in my life that something had happened that felt fictional, the kind of thing I only read about, but there she was all the same.

We walked down the steps of the tiered gardens through dipping palms and unnaturally green lawns, away from the belly-dancing waitresses and the noise of the house, and stopped a few levels above the unicorn, which was anxiously tossing its head and pulling on its bridle, its silver horn occasionally catching in the light from the sconces that had been hung in the trees.

'How are you, Iris?'

'Okay. I've been back three weeks. I got a job with Aegean Records. I'm trying not to think about Ronnie.'

Ronnie was the name of the speed metal drummer.

'You know the night I came to the hotel?'

'Iris, I have girls coming to my hotel all the time, it's hard to think . . .'

She laughed. 'Well, I was running away from Ronnie. He came home with this girl. He'd fucking forgotten I was there. The girl screams, "Who are you, get out . . ." I said, "I live here . . ." He just laughed. Then I came to your room. For some reason . . .'

Beyond the glowing garden terrace and the trees and hills beneath, the sky was black and huge. I remembered how Iris and I had talked for hours that night before she fell into a restless sleep, sometimes still speaking aloud, random words that meant something only to her.

★

I sat outside with Iris for a long while, the light from the sconces flickering as the canyon wind disturbed the trees, long and jagged shadows cast from above. I told her about my plans for this trip: a road feature with Poison for the cover, a meeting with some guy who had been corresponding with Geoff at the office and who said that he had a story about Mötley Crüe – after that I thought I'd hang around for a few days and see what else was happening: it was easy to find record companies to pick up a tab in return for an interview or live review of the endless streams of bands that they were signing.

We went back to the house where the atmosphere had changed – from the peaceful vibe of post-gig euphoria and faux desert calm, it was now on a brittle and edgy cocaine high, the noise constant but fragmented, the only thing distinguishable above cranked-up sound systems were the shouts and shrieks of rampaging partygoers. The belly-dancer waitresses were long gone, one of their serving trays was now being used to chop lines on, a group of four or five standing conspiratorially around it. Glasses and bottles were strewn about. In one corner a scorpion tank had been upturned, the sand spilling out across the carpets, the scorpions nowhere to be seen. Some guy I vaguely, generically recognised – leather trousers, cowboy boots, cutaway T-shirt, backcombed hair, in other words almost anyone I'd laid eyes on in LA in the last month – came barging into Iris from behind, shocking her and making her cry out. 'Hey!' I said, and shoved him backwards. 'What the fuck, dude,' he slurred, and stumbled away. Iris took my hand. There was a loud crash and the sound of something substantial breaking – heavy, tabletop glass maybe, coming down on flagstone – that cut right through everything and suddenly there was the unicorn, eyes flared open in panic, hooves unable to gain traction on the stone floor that led in from the upper garden terrace. Given context by the human dimensions of the room, it looked huge and strong. In fear and alarm, it skidded wildly from side to side as the people nearby tried to get out of its way, its head moving rapidly up and down, the long silver horn now loose on its forehead and flapping in front of its face, spooking it further. For a moment it seemed that it would stampede through the house, but a burly guy grabbed hold of its bridle with one hand and with the other freed the horn and threw it on the floor, and soon the lithe blonde girl was there, almost as terrified as the animal, and between the two of them they calmed the horse and led it back outside, its fear dissipating, its power gone. As it turned its head, I saw the mark where its horn had been somehow glued in place; in all of the panic and confusion it looked like a smear of dark blood on its blazing white face. Two steaming heaps of horse shit lay on the floor. 'That,' I said to Iris, 'is probably a very bad omen.' She laughed and said, 'Let's go.' As we walked through the house and into the now quiet hallway, I felt a hand land on my shoulder. I turned around.

'You are one sick puppy, buddy,' said Doc McGhee.

2. Hinterlands

I once took a flight where I sat next to a guy who said that he was a former pilot for the US military. He flew strange and beautiful development aircraft high in the upper atmosphere, where, through the luminous, unfiltered light, he could look down at the curve of the earth and feel the pull of space above him, distant and alluring. He saw things out there, he said, all of the pilots did, saw things that were to them inexplicable: shimmering lights that hurtled past their supersonic aircraft as if they were standing still; glowing discs that flew in the great void; vast shapes that seemed to use the air as camouflage, occupying the light like whales occupy the ocean. Out there, impossible things began to suggest themselves, and it was easy for the mind to drift and for time and distance to take on other meanings. Sometimes they came back down with no idea how long they had been in these upper reaches, and sometimes, once or twice maybe, guys had gone up there and never come back and no one knew why – maybe they'd been taken, or become disorientated and the planes had burned up as they exited the atmosphere, or perhaps they had simply yielded to what the pilot said felt like an almost overwhelming temptation to just point the thing upwards and go, in the same way that it was sometimes hard to stop yourself from thinking about steering your car into a freeway bridge when you were driving alone at night.

This was the story that I told Iris before she fell asleep on the other bed in my junior suite at the Hyatt. The jet lag had kicked in, begun its restless mission. I got up and pulled the heavy bedspread over Iris, flicked on the sidelight and took out my book, which was written in a perfect, affectless style that matched the glaze of sleeplessness, its characters drifting through the fog of shopping malls and parties and endless drives through the desert to Palm Springs without anything really happening to them. It felt real enough. Iris snored gently and wrapped herself deeper into the blankets. After a while, I couldn't say how long, the words began to smear on the page and I put the book down, finally sleeping as I looked across the room at the outline of Iris, curled up now and hugging a pillow to her chest.

*

The next morning at nine, Iris was outside the Hyatt beside a red convertible that her father had given her. It was one of those days that you only seemed to get in Los Angeles in the late 1980s, when you could look down from Sunset towards Century City and see the thin green line of smog below its vast cobalt sky, a nuclear sun, white and deadly, searing down on to the odd lunarscape of the city itself, bleached and dried to the colour of bones and populated only by settlers.

I still felt numbed by the heavy short sleep that had been interrupted by the phone – Iris calling from the lobby, her voice disorientating me for a moment – but it felt good to be here with her. The valet handed her the keys, and we got in. The roof of the car was down all the way; it was the last, thin weeks of summer. Iris wore a crocheted hat that left shadows like freckles on her face. We took Sunset and then Hollywood Boulevard up into the canyons and we were soon on roads that I didn't know, Iris skimming the car across them. She was a smooth driver, but as the canyon road began to curve and rise, the car suddenly spun off on to the shale at the roadside, hard up against the rock, and Iris leapt out. She bent double and puked noisily.

'Oh God,' she said. 'Oh God, sorry. I'm so sorry. I felt it coming. I drank too much last night.' She retrieved her sunglasses from the roadside and dusted them off with the corner of her skirt. She put the glasses back on and readjusted her hat. She walked around to my side of the car and opened the door. 'Can you drive?' she asked. 'I don't think I can drive.'

I shunted over and got behind the wheel of Iris's car. 'Where are we going?' I asked.

'Just follow the road,' she said, so I did, driving slowly as I became familiar with the torque.

We continued up the side of the canyon, the road almost doubling back on itself as it rose and I oversteered a few times after going into the bends too quickly. Iris barely noticed. Instead she fought her hangover, eyes closed behind her glasses, head tilted up into the breeze. 'Hmm,' she said after a while. 'Hmmm. I feel better now. A little better.' She played around with the radio. 'Do you mind driving?' she said. 'I couldn't drive at all. It always happens to me this way. My hangover comes later.'

She pulled the hat down a little further over her face, and lay back. She took off her pumps and put her bare feet up on the dash. Her toes touched the windscreen. Her ankles were slim and pale, with prominent bones. She wiggled her feet to the music. I smiled. It felt good. I hadn't even minded the puking. Iris had managed that quite nicely too. We skated down the canyon edge and then up the other side, Iris pointing the way and laughing as she did. When we came out on Los

Feliz Boulevard, Iris said, 'Just follow the exit sign for the park.'

*

It was some hours later. The city lay soundless below us. It was hard to believe that we were still a part of it. The distant ocean shimmered beneath the white sun. Closer by, under the steep lip of the observatory platform, the canyon was dotted with huge white villas half-hidden by trees and high fences. Iris pointed down at one.

'That's my father's place,' she said.

I wasn't sure if she was joking or not. 'Really, he lives there?'

'Oh yes. You know it was just luck that we ever met in New York. I was barely there for longer than you.'

I put my arm around Iris and she told me the full story of her and the speed metal drummer, a story with which I was not unfamiliar as it happened in almost every band I'd ever met. I looked down at the city, and had the very clichéd thought that it was happening right now, many hundreds of times over, in many hundreds of infinitesimally different ways. It was unavoidable. Maybe Iris read my thoughts, because she smiled sadly and wiped her eyes. She didn't seem to have that bad of a case of it, even though she'd followed him to New York and back.

'So how did your old man get all that money then? He must be a music journalist too . . .' She almost smiled. 'Or porno. He makes legendary skin flicks in the Valley . . .'

She almost giggled. 'No, he wanted to be a boxer, but he started selling cars. Then he bought a car lot, and then another, then he started making real-estate deals or something . . .'

'Yeah?'

'Yeah,' she said. 'He's bought and sold most of Sherman Oaks. You know the Galleria out there? He had that land for a while.'

'I don't feel sorry for you any more. I feel sorry for the drummer. He's thrown away a bankroll.'

She smiled again, less sadly this time. 'It's been a nice day,' she said.

As darkness fell Iris drove us back through the canyons to Hollywood; she drove fast and in perfect control, flipping the car around the hairpins with practised ease. I told her about the dinner I had to go to at a place called the Blue Room where I was supposed to meet a guy named Donald who had been writing and calling the editor of the magazine for weeks, telling him he had a story that would shock the world. Geoff had taken a malicious delight in sending me down there – and he knew it would be the kind of thing I wouldn't blow out because I was too drunk or bombed or hanging out with Lemmy at the Rainbow for the ninth night in a row. He understood that I had the same itch for new things that he once had.

'Iris,' I said. 'Would you like to go on a date?'

★

We walked into the studied dark of the Blue Room and I saw him right away, at the back, on his own.

'I'm Donald,' he said.

'Hey Donald, this is Iris. Did you bring it?'

'Yes,' he said, and slid a package across the table. His hand shook as he did it. I pushed my hand inside the envelope and took out a transparent plastic folder filled with pictures and a lawyer's brief drawn together with string. Iris moved the candle on the table closer. She put her thigh flat against mine.

'This is gonna blow your fuckin' mind,' said Donald.

Iris giggled. 'Ooh, is it,' she said.

I laughed, but Donald didn't. He was like something out of an Elmore Leonard novel, indeterminately middle-aged with a burned-out hippy vibe, his hair greased back, his finger-nails broad and quick-bitten. He began a long and pedantic monologue, his face uplit by the flame of the candle, all deep lines and shadows. Donald was from Florida, he ran a company that sold surveillance devices by mail order from a house in the margins of the Everglades. Once a fortnight he'd drive up the coast in an old pick-up to Sarasota, where he shared office space with a retired cop who did low-rent private-investigation work: small businessmen with beefs; paranoid wives of local big shots; feuding neighbours and their parking disputes. They'd been sitting there in the office one Thursday morning, drinking coffee and trying to work out a way to make more money more easily when a silly-looking kid with teased-up hair and jeans tucked inside of his cowboy boots – they were seeing more and more of them on the streets with all this MTV shit on the whole time – came through the door wanting to know how he might record both sides of a telephone conversation. It was pretty simple if you had sixty bucks for one of the two-way microphones that Donald sold and a tape recorder to plug it into, but they decided they'd have a little fun with this kid first. Donald pulled a form from a drawer and told him that he'd have to fill out all the details of the number that he wanted to record so that he could apply for a state licence to do so, and they'd been laughing under their breath and trying not to hoot out loud until the kid started talking.

★

Iris fiddled with the string that held the lawyer's brief together. Her hands were quite beautiful; thin wrists and long and slender fingers. Her thigh remained against mine. Something was happening, who knew what. A ghostly waiter floated up, pouring wine into big glasses. Donald stopped speaking while the ghost was there and started again when he'd gone. 'So this kid says he has a friend who's been in jail,' he said. 'He's held up a liquor store, something stupid like that. The guy's out now, and he says he's got a lot of money coming if he can figure out a way to get it.

'Well you know half the guys in jail think they've got money coming when they get out. But this one's different. Turns out he's been in a rock band, and this band do have quite a bit of money, and some of it should be his . . .'

Donald paused again while the waiter floated back through the shadows. We ordered some food. Donald wasn't the kind of guy who was going to hurry with his story. He tapped his fingers on top of the plastic folder and watched the waiter drift off.

'. . . We say, okay, you come back here tomorrow together, and maybe we can help. I figured they'd probably never show, but next day, they did, and in walked Matthew.'

Donald spoke about Matthew with something like love. He was tall, tan, his jail haircut growing out, his hair dyed jet black again. He looked like a fucking rock star with his razored cheekbones and sweeping jawline. No wonder all the small-town kids were talking about him: Matthew Trippe was like an alien among them, and when Donald had listened to his story and asked what proof he had that it was true, Matt had simply rolled up the sleeve of his denim shirt to reveal an armful of ornate and expensive tattoos that had probably cost more than Donald paid for a half-year rental on his crappy little office. Matt had a wife and a kid and no job so Donald took him on pro bono. All they had was in these folders. I opened the transparent one and set some pictures out on the table.

★

Iris had driven me back to the hotel and left me there. All of the tiredness of the last few days had folded around me and I'd slept heavily before the jet lag pulled me back up through its fathoms, so now I sat with Donald's photos and magazine clippings spread all over the bed. He had talked for what seemed like hours – in fact it *was* hours – his food barely touched while Iris and I ate and listened, and the only time he had stopped was when it came to the bill, at which point he disappeared to the restroom and didn't come out. In the end Iris had reached into her bag and pulled out her record-company plastic. She raised her eyebrows at me.

'Don't worry, Iris,' I'd said. 'I'll . . .' and she raised her eyebrows again.

'You'll what?' Iris said. 'No . . . you'll do whatever I tell you,' and then she'd smirked. Finally Donald returned from the restroom. I noticed as he slipped between the tables with their flickering candles that he had a strange stoop and a limp. He looked pretty old and beaten down. He took out a business card that had a little picture of him looking at least thirty years younger on it, and pushed it into my hand. I promised to call him as soon as I got back into town.

'Goodnight, Ellis,' he'd said to Iris, and neither of us could say anything more until he'd walked from the room, when we'd doubled up into helpless laughter.

On the way back to the Hyatt we joked about him planting

one of his listening devices in Iris's car, but now, in the oppressive quiet of the hotel late at night, it wasn't quite as funny, or as unlikely. Donald was a weird guy, and the story laid out on the bed was fragmented and rambling with lots of ragged edges and untied ends, but it had been obsessively compiled. It had the feel of deeply haunted truth. The story was a simple one, yet insistent and relevant because the band that it concerned, Mötley Crüe, were big and getting inexorably bigger, and what's more had defined much of the iconography of the Sunset Strip scene with the way they looked, sounded and lived. Matthew said that, following a catastrophic and debilitating car accident involving their bass player and main songwriter Nikki Sixx, he had been recruited into the band, assuming Sixx's name, identity and role for more than a year as they became increasingly famous and well rewarded, as they cut records and went on tour and appeared on television, until their manager, who happened to be Doc McGhee, discarded him, ruthlessly and without a penny, once the original Nikki had recovered.

It was strange and unlikely, something that added to the feeling I had that nothing here was certain. I knew I should leave it alone, call Matthew a flake and get out, but I wasn't going to. The story of a lost kid who by genetic fluke looked enough like a badly fucked-up rock star to slip into his band and take his place, the change unnoticed by anyone until his own life became so chaotic that he too was covertly replaced – I couldn't even begin to explain the feeling that it aroused in me, a sense of inchoate mayhem that nonetheless had an irresistible appeal.

I had interviewed Mötley Crüe once, in London. They'd arrived in four separate limousines that parked one behind the other outside. The cars had brought them straight from the airport. They'd been in Japan, where things had gone badly – an incident on a bullet train when a full bottle of whiskey was thrown at a salaryman's head; a band member discovered bruised and disorientated in a Tokyo street late one night; the remaining dates hastily cancelled with a bland and implausible excuse – and they were in Europe for two days of press before returning to America, where their latest record, they had just been informed in a fax sent by Doc, would debut at number two on the Billboard chart with sales of half a million in its first week.

They had no real idea where they were or what they were doing. They were surrounded by employees who took them to places, introduced them to people, whispered in their ears why they were there and what might happen next. This great vagueness, along with the accompanying smear of jet lag and the disconcerting constancy of identical hotel rooms in different cities night after night, month upon month, made them seem even more detached and isolated than they might otherwise have been. I gained only the loosest impression of them in our hours together. Mick Mars was the strangest. He was small and stooped and at least ten years older than the rest of the band, the layers of white powder he had on his face unable to hide its deep lines. The skin on his hands was dry and thin, his knuckles bulbous and stiff. His hair was dyed a shade so black it was almost blue. He stared straight forwards no matter who was talking to him or what he was looking at, and he said almost nothing in the two hours we were together, except at the very start when I shouted my name in his ear three times as an introduction. 'Hey bud . . .' he eventually croaked, his voice no more than an arid whisper. 'Just spacin' . . .'

Vince Neil was short too, blond, hyperactively twitchy and

with a fragile cocaine-like attention span, his eyes constantly flitting around the room. He seemed preoccupied with how he looked, flicking his hair out so it fell properly down the back of his jacket and examining himself in the mirror every few minutes (as he did so, I thought of something that another musician had said to me, in bitterly aggressive tones, one night at the Rainbow: 'Get a photograph of Vince, take a black marker pen and colour in his hair and his eyebrows and you'll see what he really is – a fucking Mexican'). If Mick was mysterious, at least in his strangeness, Vince was pretty easy to read, a narcissistic hedonist who had, by his own estimation, slept with 'thousands' of women, and was on to his second marriage, a recent union with a mudwrestler from an infamous LA club called the Tropicana. In many ways Vince was lucky, because he had no discernible talent (his rangeless voice struggled with even the most basic of melodies), but he looked good on stage and in the band's videos, and was a cipher for the dreams and aspirations of every kid seeking a break on the Sunset Strip: if Vince could make it then so could they, so could anyone.

Life seemed to be indulging Vince to an epic degree; cars, girls, money, anything he wanted, and his irresponsibility was equally epic. He had found himself in a position where nothing he did held any consequences for him; even when he drunkenly crashed his car and killed his passenger, a drummer called Razzle from the Finnish band Hanoi Rocks, and badly injured the occupants of an oncoming vehicle, he staggered clear of the wreckage uninjured and somehow served just nineteen days in jail despite being convicted of vehicular manslaughter.

There was a darkness to Vince, in his endless solipsism, that was missing in Tommy, the drummer, even though to the outsider their lifestyles would appear identical. Tommy had just got married too (it seemed like just another thing to do for them, just another way to keep life moving along) to Heather Locklear, a hot, famous TV actress whom Tommy had asked out on a whim thinking that she was actually someone else, but judging by the story he told his bandmates, loudly, while we all stood around, Heather was already complaining about another woman that Tommy swore he hadn't been seeing.

'Man,' Vince said to him, 'that's a bummer, getting busted for a boner you never even had . . .'

If sex was Tommy's thing, then drugs were Nikki Sixx's. And if Vince's darkness came from the havoc he caused others, then Nikki's was of a far bleaker and more nihilistic kind. He was in the grip of a deep, self-medicating heroin addiction (who knew what pain it hid; being one of the biggest rock stars in America wasn't enough to end it), and because he had money, he was shielded from the usual physical and mental decline that came with long-term opiate use. Nonetheless, there were horrifying stories in circulation: a messy OD on Valentine's Day before a gig in London, the panicky dealer hitting him repeatedly with a baseball bat to bring him round; another in LA, where he slipped so far into unconsciousness his heart briefly stopped.

He was in a foul mood, with me ('you write shitty things') and with everyone else, and he had a heavy, brooding presence that affected the entire room. Part of that was his size – he was tall, well over six feet, and where Tommy was rock-star skinny, Nikki was thickset and had the shoulders and arms of a much stronger man – but mostly it came from an attitude that suggested he could do anything at any time. He clearly ran the band. He wrote the songs, came up with the artwork concepts, the way they looked and the way they dressed. The others deferred to him almost automatically, so when he said that they would do the interview in pairs, first Vince and Tommy and then he and Mick, they simply sat and did as they were told, as docile as cattle, Tommy sunny and telling funny stories about the Japanese tour, Vince bored and distracted, urgently seeking something to alleviate the tedium of all of this and keen just to go home (he reacted with undisguised horror when Tommy reminded him that Doc was planning some shows in Russia), Mick wordless and still staring forwards, Nikki glowering and resentful, the muscles in his jaw bunching as he clenched his teeth together.

I turned on the TV to feel less alone. The sunlit uplands of the observatory seemed days rather than hours, distant. I woke up some time later with the morning news blaring and a couple of Donald's photocopies stuck to my face. Glamour was not dead.

*

In the lobby of the Hyatt, there was a scene that seemed dreamlike, or filmic, or at least novelistic and created: scores of people were standing in its very small space, and even more people, mostly girls, were outside, pushed up against the glass of the full-length windows, desperate to see whoever they thought was inside. The concierge was looking nervous, occasionally shrieking at the porters and the bellboys who were trying to wrangle case-laden trollies towards the lifts. The heat was oppressive, the humming air con simply recycling it unpleasantly, the smell emanating from it sharp and male. The reason for all of this was Poison, the proto-hair metal party band whose new record was selling 200,000 copies a week, whose videos were on heavy rotation on MTV, whose brand of disposable, deliberately trashy rock 'n' roll had all the gravitas of candyfloss, but was right now, by whatever cosmic fluke, the soundtrack to half a million Friday nights. The dreams they sold were dreams of escape. They had caught a wave of their own making, and now they were playing 15,000-seat sheds six nights a week as they criss-crossed America, grossing, according to the figures I checked in Boxscore, around $450,000 per show. The magazine wanted its cover story so we were picking up the tour in LA – Long Beach Arena, another boiling shed, sold out months ago – and travelling on to San Diego and New Mexico.

I was getting into my usual mood when going on a job, that of not wanting to go, hoping for some kind of unlikely last-gasp reprieve, perhaps the chance to see Iris instead, drive somewhere in her car and talk about the weirdness of last night, when I felt a hand on my shoulder, and from the crowd a vision emerged. It was Ray. He was a photographer with the magazine. We often travelled together. He'd been in the business twenty years before I met him. In the smiting light and early heat he looked like a vampire, his skin sallow and stretched across his face, his teeth the same colour as his skin, his hair dry and thinning, a cigarette trapped in his long fingers. He was wearing what he always wore, a tight denim shirt open almost to the waist, drainpipe jeans and white Dunlop trainers that in the evenings he sometimes exchanged for cowboy boots. Before his first drink of the day, there was a brittleness to his speech and his movements that was noticeable only to those who knew him well. He was accomplished at masking it like the most practised are, but the morning was too bright and he'd been doing it for too long; the sun scorched his blasted retinas and pulled a line of moisture over his top lip, and he had to keep his head turned away from the source of the light. 'Hello, darling,' he said to me – he called everyone, male and female, darling, one of his many endearing habits – and all of a sudden it felt better to be here, with someone familiar, an accomplice on the journey.

We escaped the throng and stewed in the heat of the Hyatt car park while Ray smoked a cigarette until at last the band came down and the tour bus opened its doors. A few minutes later it threaded its way on to Sunset, the shouts and cries of the crowd outside the hotel silenced by the thick tinted glass. We sat high above them, looking down, expressionless. The band stayed away from the windows until we'd merged into the traffic, headed downtown, and then they fell easily into the roles assigned for them: Rikki the hyperactive, lovable drummer; Bobby the almost silent, stoic bass player; CC the zonked-out, dumb-blond guitarist; and Bret the heroic, handsome, funny singer.

I thought about the other times I'd interviewed them: once, desultorily, in the Rainbow as they released their self-financed debut record (them trying so desperately hard to please, me distracted by other things); a car-crash of a phoner with a stoned and barely audible CC when that same album, against all odds, went platinum; a valedictory follow-up with Bret, the tables between us turned for ever now; then a thirty-minute face-to-face in a suite at the Landmark in London last winter, them just off the plane, pale with jet lag and cold, trying hard but barely present.

They couldn't really remember, and I didn't expect or want them too. Ray and I were just people who appeared in front of them at random intervals like lots of others, wanting something, wanting anything, and who after a while simply merged together into the general blur. Once the bus got going we all relaxed; the usual codes were in place, the main one being that what happened on tour, stayed on tour. CC made a couple of discreet trips to his bunk area. Bret grabbed some dumb-bells and worked out in the lounge, grunting effortfully. Rikki flipped through some motorcycle magazines. Bobby was nowhere to be seen. Duggie, the tour manager, came and sat with us and told funny stories. He slid a tape into the VCR and showed us some of the films he'd shot on the road: lines of giggling Japanese girls in school uniform; CC naked and unconscious in a hotel corridor; a guy who had each of the band's faces tattooed on his arms and chest; rolls and rolls of banknotes being rammed into bags, the merchandising take from a single night somewhere in Russia that they'd been unable to take out of the country, so instead had reinvested in some oil fields in the Siberian steppes.

CC came and joined us, rubbing his eyes and yawning loudly. 'Dude, watch this, it's that chick I was telling you about,' he mumbled to Duggie, and took a tape from a shelf by the VCR, ejecting Duggie's and pushing his own into the machine. After a few moments of static and noise, a grimy, unsteady picture settled on the screen as harsh sounds – stiletto heels on a hard floor, objects being hurriedly dropped, a guy's voice, too distorted to make out clearly – squeezed through the tinny speakers rigged to the TV. The images lurched queasily as the video camera was screwed on to a tripod and aimed at a futon thrown on the floor. An ornate crucifix hung above it on an otherwise bare wall. It filled with shadow as from out of shot on the right came a girl, naked, dark-eyed, who stared straight down the lens before blowing a kiss.

CC watched for a while and said, 'I want to get a better video camera. This guy I know at MTV said he'd get me a more pro set-up,' and I could see right then that the band had passed from the years of saying no to the years of saying yes – there was no midpoint in this transition, no years of saying maybe or perhaps, just a border crossing at which all of the answers to their questions changed, when all of the club owners and booking agents and record companies and hotel clerks and car salesmen and shop assistants and liquor stores and drug dealers and girls who had always said no suddenly started saying yes. There was a further stage, rarer, more distant still, where questions ceased to be posed; they were instead anticipated, granted before they ever arose, but CC was at the moment infatuated by 'yes'. It would be, I guessed, a couple of years before 'no' became the only interesting answer, respite from getting everything that he wanted. I watched him. He was short, with tiny girlish hands and a big nose, a dried omelette of bleached blond hair virtually doubling the size of his head. On the screen, his bare arse bobbed up and down as he fucked the girl, his voice, processed by the speakers into a gimmicky, robot babble, urging another girl, now in shot, to take off the T-shirt she was wearing and join them, and as she did, Bret and Ray came into the cabin and slumped down next to us on the sofa. We watched in silence.

'Bro,' Bret said to CC after a while, 'you really need to get some furniture.'

*

We drove downtown through South Central past heat-scarred lo-rises and immigrant stores. Aside from the bright sun on white streets this was a new and different city. CC's porno finished and Ray corralled everyone at the back of the bus and shot casual pictures while I did an interview – their glorious lives, the triumphant new album (better even than the last one), the enemies they had vanquished. We talked about their influences – the Who, the Stones, the New York Dolls, Tchaikovsky, Kerouac, Faulkner, Francis Ford Coppola, *Straw Dogs*, *Breakfast at Tiffany's*, *Top Gun* – their love for 'the kids' that had besieged the hotel foyer and the millions of others like them out there in America. CC spoke for ten minutes about his 'deep connection' to the blues as he wrote a song called 'I Want Action'. I think Bret at one point mentioned Frank Lloyd Wright. I asked the questions that allowed them to give these answers.

The interview killed time for a while, but as the traffic slowed a torpor settled on the bus. For all of its luxury it was too small, too hot, too slow. The band had done this for two years, stopped to make an album and now they were doing it for another two years. They accepted its lulls, didn't fight them. The bus might usually have been full of women, but LA was the classic girlfriends show, the one they always wanted to come to. Bret was seeing a girl called Pamela, who had just been on the cover of *Playboy*. Bobby and CC had girlfriends too. Rikki the drummer had several. Finally we reached Long Beach.

The arena was huge and empty. Local crew were loading chairs into the stalls. The band soundchecked while Ray and I stood in the wings. The girlfriends arrived. People milled around. Pamela was absurdly beautiful and it distanced her; she and Bret together glowed, a different species to the rest of us. Ray had arranged to shoot more pictures down on the beach, so we walked out of the arena and through the loading bay, unseen by the fans already gathering in the parking lots, and down towards the sea, strung out in twos and threes in the last of the day's sun, the heat rising from the pavements, the breeze sweet and autumnal, our stretching shadows black against the white stone. The sand was still warm too, and we walked unhurriedly along it until the arena and the docks grew hazy behind us and in front came the great wide reaches of Long Beach, without the faded romance of Venice, not as moneyed and remote as Malibu, but instead vast and arcane. Ray set the band with their backs to the sun and began to photograph them. They looked different now, not the road-weary, venal residents of the tour bus, instead young, rich, tanned, blessed, chosen. They finished up and Bret asked Ray if he would shoot some pictures of him with Pamela, who, in the light of the low sun and with the wind in her hair looked like an image on a movie screen, too perfect to be here amongst us. The others turned and began to head back up the beach.

Behind Bret and Pamela, way in the distance, a driftwood fire burned. Ray had me holding a silver reflector as he shot. After each roll of film, Pamela removed more clothes. Soon she was down to a bikini. Bret took off his shirt and undid the top buttons on his jeans. They entwined, kissed, practically made out. They were obviously heavily into one another, it was almost embarrassing to be there.

'Now I need you a little apart, darlings,' Ray said, and he managed to separate them for a last roll. I knew what he was doing; craftily banging off a few of Pamela without Bret. She was probably wise to it, but went along with him anyway. The minute he stopped, a light in her went out. She looked like a girl again. She bent down and gathered up her clothes. It didn't feel right to watch her put them back on. I helped Ray repack his kit.

'Thanks, man,' Bret said to him. 'I can get those pictures, right?'

'Sure,' Ray said, and Bret took Pamela's hand and began walking up the beach. By the time Ray was ready to go, they were small figures in the distance. We headed out after them, the evening breeze stiffening, street lights along the shoreline beginning to appear. After a few minutes a figure from the group ahead began to fall back towards us, and we soon caught up. It was Martha, one of the girlfriends. Martha was sweet and funny and wan, and what she wanted to know was whether we had seen her man with another woman, whom she described in detail, and there was something ineffably sad both about the question and the way she waited to ask it.

*

The girlfriends didn't come to San Diego. The bus filled with women. Ray gave Bret the pictures of him and Pamela. He showed me the half-roll he'd squeezed out of Pamela on her own. They were sensational: the descending sun, the endless sand, the distant beacon of the driftwood fire.

In New Mexico I tried twice to call Iris, but missed her both times. We caught a plane back to LA and re-checked into the Hyatt. Iris had left me a postcard at the desk. It was a fake picture of an alien sitting on the Hollywood sign. She'd drawn a speech bubble coming from its mouth that said 'I am Donald' and on the back 'Call me now – love Ellis'.

3. Haunted Coast

Doc McGhee had a drug problem. He didn't take them. He imported them into America. He got busted bringing 29,000 lb of marijuana into North Carolina.

The words swam a little in front of my eyes. I was back in my room. It was late and I was waiting for Iris to return my call. Ray was probably still downstairs in the bar, where we'd sat for an hour watching the lounge act, a guy in a tux on an electric keyboard and a once-beautiful girl resigning herself to singing Christopher Cross songs in chain hotels. Then they stopped and walked to separate ends of the room to drink, neither so much as looking at the other. Ray had that glassy stillness he always got when he was drunk, the only outward sign and that only apparent when you knew him well, and for some reason I got a vision of him being somewhere like this in ten years' time doing exactly the same thing so I'd finished my beer and left him to it. I picked up a package at reception and inside were some copies of the magazine, already out in England, with a story I'd written just before I'd left about Doc's drug bust. It was why he'd approached me at the party just after the unicorn had taken a dump on the floor. Somehow he'd seen it days before I had, which was mildly alarming. As I read it, I thought of Doc's hand on my shoulder, his voice in my ear, in the hallway, with Iris holding my hand: 'You are one sick puppy, buddy.'

I'm sick? Well you imported the drugs, buddy.

The spirit of the stairway, the thing I should have said. I hadn't though. With the clatter of the party heavy in nearby rooms, the spooked unicorn still in my mind, Iris's hand in mine, I'd wondered for a second what the hell he was talking about, and then when I realised I'd given an uncertain laugh and walked off before he could say any more, although I heard him shouting something that sounded like, 'Oh yeah, oh yeah, bye bye, buddy, bye bye . . .'

Now his face came back to me again, a fat guy's face, a bad guy's face. The colour of walnut. White, white teeth. Smiling Doc. Papa Doc. The music business came easy to guys like Doc. When you thought about it, it was a lot like the drugs business. It was all logistics. You had to source your product then get it in front of the people who wanted it. That's what Doc did. And once you'd negotiated in the drugs business, walking into the office of the CEO of Sony Records and telling him that he had to give you another half a million dollars hardly held any fears. It was all you could do to stop yourself from laughing as the sweat spread across his top lip and he organised the cheque.

The drugs business and the music business had always been connected. Doc was just one of the threads that joined them. Having a band on the road was a good way to wash your money, too. The music business was a cash business, the fees, the wages, the merchandise.

Doc had started out small, but now he had two of the biggest bands in America, Mötley Crüe and Bon Jovi. He broke them by keeping them on the road, taking the product to the people, city after city, month after month, year after year. Doc worked as hard as they did, and somehow he also managed to lend his services to a drug-importation ring. There had always been rumours about Doc, but then there were rumours about lots of people. It wasn't until a shrimping boat with a wooden hull called the *Lady Mauricette*, out of Wilmington, North Carolina, was found to be carrying thirteen tons of primo-grade dope that someone finally pulled on the thread.

★

It wasn't hard to imagine what had happened. On that vast and often empty coast, where the land was flat and windblown beyond, the Beaufort Inlet was one of three natural estuaries in North Carolina that could be used in all weathers, but it was a dangerous and mournful place, part of a region that every boater knows as the Graveyard of the Atlantic, and the town of Beaufort, popular with tourists, had a ghost walk with a guide who told stories of the drowned and the lost, their bodies never returned by the water. No one knew quite how many ships had sunk there, disorientated by the sudden sea fogs, dragged on to the sandbars by the strong and unpredictable currents, but it was more than 600. Thousands more sailed over the dead.

It was the fourth of July weekend 1982, and there were still white horses on the water as the sun went down and the pleasure boats that had been out all day headed back towards the lights and bars of Beaufort and Morehead City. A wooden shrimper called the *Bobby M* came in from Cape Lookout and was headed south towards Cape Fear when the coastguard decided to run a routine registration check and discovered that the boat wasn't called the *Bobby M* at all but the *Lady Mauricette*, and when they got it into the harbour at Morehead City, they found the false hull and the hidden refrigeration section and the 29,000 lb of Colombian marijuana. The story that I had written and that the magazine had just published outlined these moments and went on to precis, in a couple of thousand words, the dramatic events of the next five years: the investigation and arrest of the three men at the centre of the operation, a playboy from Grand Cayman called Leigh Ritch, who sourced the supply, Stephen Kalish from Houston, who ran the transport chain, and Mike Vogel of Detroit, a street guy with the connections to sell vast quantities of drugs, and the fallout afterwards; the heavily guarded house in Tampa with millions of dollars of cash inside; the connection forged between Kalish and General Manuel Noriega, leader of Panama's ruling military junta; the Panamanian banks that they filled with money; the Lear jet that Kalish bought to fly Noriega to a meeting with President Reagan and then on to Las Vegas for a week of partying; the launch of the US government's 'War on Drugs'; the cruise ship that hosted a week-long party to celebrate the successful arrival of 'the mother load' of 50,000 tons of dope; the internal power struggle that led to Vogel ordering the shooting of the gang's head of security; their infiltration by the FBI and the eventual indictment of 185 people, including Doc, who had provided their start-up finance and who was named by Kalish as the link between the gang and a Colombian drug supplier.

Doc had just pleaded guilty to involvement in the North Carolina bust and been given a suspended sentence on the grounds that he was now 'fully committed' to spreading an anti-drug message through his 'high profile in the music business', had raised the money for an MTV documentary about their dangers and was establishing the 'Make a Difference'

Foundation to organise the Moscow Peace Festival at which all of his bands would play.

★

'I told my father about you. He wants to meet you. We can go to his beach house this weekend, if you're free.'

Iris was back. Her little red car was parked downstairs and we were on the roof of the Hyatt by the rippling pool. She held the stem of her glass steady on the rail, bobbing the ice cubes up and down with the long fingers of her free hand and listening as I talked about Doc and the magazine story. I had barely slept, or at least it felt that way. Instead I had endured a gnawing early-hours paranoia, my mind inventing increasingly extreme yet increasingly likely scenarios involving the repercussions from writing about Doc's drug bust, vindictive ways in which he might destroy me professionally or personally or both: banning me from interviewing any of his bands; turning PRs and label executives against me; demanding that the magazine fire me if it wanted continued access to his acts and shows; spreading disruptive rumours ('Oh well, you know about *that guy*, right . . . ?'); suing me; having me followed and scared off; planting drugs on me at the airport; even, at one point, thinking about kids who go missing in the deserts around LA, about all of those others lost at sea ('Yeah, it's kinda weird – he was supposed to meet the band, but he never showed. Haven't seen him for days . . .'). 'Disappear here', just like the giant hoardings advertising LA along Sunset said. I realised it was ludicrous as soon as I woke, and Iris giggled as I told her, but then she'd said that perhaps it would be a good idea to get out of the city for a couple of days and invited me to go and visit her father at his place on the coast.

By six, Iris and I were on the freeway. By seven, the sea was to our right, the hinterland to the left. The roof was down. Iris took off her shoes and put her feet up on the dash. Her skirt was short. I could see her panties. I felt shallow and transparent. The city and its people slipped away in the rear-view mirror, and in what seemed like moments we were at Iris's father's place, a deco-inspired mansion set high on a bluff above the water amongst towering garden palms with a shimmering pool and a deck dug out of the cliff with un-interrupted views of the ocean that stretched out to the distant horizon.

Iris fell into her daddy's arms. I shook his hand. It was broad and thick. Her father had a woman in the city and one on the coast. Tonight, it was the one from the coast. Her name was Sherry. She sat out on the deck, manning the small pool bar. She was Iris's age, and she kind of looked like Iris would if Iris had been poor and on the make. Sherry was fun. She drank too much and squeezed Iris's father's balls through his shorts when she thought we weren't looking. Iris caught his eye and smiled at him. I smiled too. I started to feel a little drunk, from the wine and the house and the view.

*

Iris and her father announced that they would cook dinner. Sherry and I sat on the deck and watched the ocean darken as we drank. My appetite sharpened. From the kitchen came clanks, clunks, howls, laughs, screams, shrieks, bangs and hisses. An hour passed. Sherry and I had run out of conversation. Iris and her father brought out hot plates loaded with food. They dropped them on the table and headed back to the kitchen. As they went through the door, Iris's father couldn't resist slapping Iris on the ass. Iris squealed and laughed and jumped forwards into the house.

'Jesus,' said Sherry, and lit a cigarette.

The dinner went on. Iris and her father came out and sat down for bursts of eating before disappearing back inside again. Then they'd be out with more heaped plates. We ate lobster and crayfish, prawns, squid, octopus, sea snails. They were all drenched in sauces and butters. Iris poured us out big glasses of chilled wine. The food was sensual. I picked it up, let the butter run down my fingers. I pushed heaped chunks of lobster flesh into my mouth. I could feel and smell it as well as taste it: all that good life snuffed out and served up. Iris's father was a sensualist, too. He ate with his hands, pulling and cracking and shelling. Iris was barely more delicate.

As we ate, we exclaimed:

'Oh yes!'

'My God!'

'This's beautiful . . .'

'Mmmm–oh!'

'More!'

It felt so good we laughed in happiness. Iris had moistened lips, a loose piece of shell like a beauty spot to the left of her nose, no make-up. She tore at the food. She spoke with her mouth full. She wiped her hands on the tablecloth. She was a wonder, a force of nature with the great night sea behind her. I zoned out of the conversation and I thought about Iris. She had seemed rudderless and tumbling when I first knew her, apparently fazed by the world outside of houses like this one and the other gated compound we'd looked down on from the observatory that day, but now she seemed firm and assured. She had shrugged off the drummer, was no longer teary and wistful, instead decisive and capable, wry and wise.

The meal finished late. Sherry gave up and left us to it. Iris's father fell asleep at the table with his head back and his mouth open. Iris put him to bed.

★

The house had a guest chalet, partly hidden at the end of a stone path on which tiny lizards basked until they felt approaching footsteps. Iris and I stayed in there – I guessed her father didn't want Iris and me too close to him and Sherry. The chalet had a kitchen, a lounge and a bedroom, all in white, with another sweeping, moonlit vista of the ocean beyond. Iris came to bed in just her panties, running shyly in from the bathroom, covering her breasts with her hands. Iris was beautiful, pale skin and long legs. 'Where are those pyjamas?' I asked, and she laughed. We began to kiss. After a while, she rolled away.

'No?' I said.

'No,' she replied. 'No, not yet.'

She fell asleep in my arms. I stroked the top of her head and listened to the nightbirds screech.

★

We spent the next day by the pool. Iris wore a white bikini. Sherry looked hot too, but obvious. Iris's father kept eyeing her. He and I lay back in the sun and thought good things about the world. Iris and Sherry splashed in the water. They could have been sisters. I wondered if Iris had noticed. We all swam together. Iris's father fondled Sherry under the water. I wanted to grab Iris, but I held back. He was testing me and I knew it. Iris's father and I got out of the pool. As we dried off in the blades of light streaming through the palms, I said: 'Sherry's fun.'

'There's a world full of Sherrys.'

'Maybe, if you can find them.'

'Oh, they'll find you, son. The trick is to know when to say no.'

'No to what?'

'Just "no".'

'So Sherry's not the one, then?'

'I don't think any one is the one. Have more than one.'

'I don't think that Iris thinks that I'm the one, either.'

Iris's father didn't reply, but I was glad that I had got it out.

We looked at the girls in the pool once more. The sun had swung around behind them and haloed, in silhouette, they were impossible to tell apart.

*

That night Iris drove us back to LA, down through the darkening hills and on to the freeway, its looming overpasses ominous now in the nightfall, horsetails visible on the wind-whipped ocean. We barely spoke as she pushed the red car towards the city. Almost no one passed on the other side of the median. For the first time in a while, the place appeared alien, lunar, and it wasn't until the traffic began to thicken and houses started to appear on the hills that the feeling began to lift. Soon the roads glowed with the lights of the city, and we headed up through Costa Mesa and Huntingdon Beach, Seal Beach and Long Beach, and then inland to Lomita and Torrance, Iris certain and strong again, and in no time we were back on the Strip, passing the Cat & Fiddle and the Roxy and the Rainbow, the traffic slowing as the signals above Sunset turned red and green and red, she and I looking over at the kids walking up and down and handing out their flyers. I began to wonder whether anything between us had changed, but just before Iris went to make a right into the Hyatt, she turned to me and said, 'Okay then, your place or mine?'

4. *Fountain Avenue*

I wrote up the Poison story I owed the magazine at the table in Iris's kitchen on a typewriter that the Hyatt had loaned me on the condition it didn't leave the hotel, and that we'd sneaked out under a white towel while trying not to laugh or drop it. It took a couple of days, and Iris faxed the copy to London from her office. I had a long conversation with Geoff about the pieces he wanted me to work on – something on Matthew Trippe as soon as I could do it; to meet up with an English singer who'd relocated to LA with her band for the summer; and a couple of fillers on acts whose record companies would pick up the tab for the hotel – in all it would buy me two or three weeks in the city without worrying about flying back. I kept the room on at the Hyatt, and Iris dropped me there on her way to work so that I could make phone calls and sit by the pool with Ray while he got slowly smashed as we checked out the women who spent their languid hours there.

Iris's place was a large Spanish-style casa with a giant, decaying palm in the garden on a quiet road off Fountain Avenue, at the end where West Hollywood tailed out into Silver Lake. She shared it with three other girls, two of whom sold ad space at the *Recycler* and never seemed to be home, only occasionally slipping in and out of the deeply shaded rooms to eat or change or pack bags of clothes, tied up in their lives and plans with boyfriends and gigs and movies. The other was Brenna, older, a family friend of Iris's for many years, who worked as a PA somewhere in Century City and who was also running a sideline as a beautician – 'fanny-waxer to the stars' as she called herself – telling us indiscreet stories about the body-hair disasters of almost-famous TV actresses. There were hints of some kind of dark personal crisis that had brought Brenna here – a parting, a loss – and I saw her standing alone under the palm in the early-morning cool, smoking cigarettes, her robe pulled tight around her.

I got back a couple of afternoons later to find a note that said 'Party next door'. I walked around. It was an almost identical house that had also a pool out back with an owner who worked overseas and relied on Brenna to look after the place. There were cars parked askew on either side of the driveway and some music coming in a dampened thud from inside the house. Brenna answered the door in a bikini top and a sarong. She looked great; full and heavy, ripe. She was tanned, out of all those office clothes.

'Come in.'

'Thanks.'

'We're by the pool.'

'Great.'

'Iris is here.'

Iris was dressed identically to Brenna. She looked great, too. She hugged me. It felt good. We smiled. Brenna found me a drink. She slid away. Her broad hips swung. Iris told me about all of the people at the party. Some were from the little record label that she worked for (easy to spot in their free band T-shirts and studied cool) but most were friends of hers and Brenna's.

I sat in a chair by the pool. The party guests shrieked and laughed and talked. Iris came and sat with me. She was drinking some kind of elaborate punch from a tall glass. After a while, Brenna joined us too and she and Iris began pointing out some of the guests gathered around the pool, aspiring actresses mostly whom Brenna knew through her hair-removal business.

'Great legs.'

'She's gorgeous, but she's a flake.'

'Nice shoes.'

'Big ass.'

'I'd like tits like that; tits that size.'

'Underneath that swimsuit,' said Brenna, 'that girl is hairier than a monkey . . .'

Iris dipped in the pool, and so did Brenna. I knew I was doomed to think of them together. I got another drink and sat there as the sun swung around towards the hills.

I needed the bathroom. Iris directed me. Through the house, up the stairs, third left, white door. It was closed. I tried the handle and the door moved. I had the wrong door. Brenna was standing behind it, changing. Her clothes were on her bed. She had on just a dark blue thong. Her breasts were full and low, her nipples puckered by the water. Her hair was wet and unbrushed. She had stretch marks on her stomach and thighs. She was magnificent, a comet at the end of its run. Age might soon have her, but not yet. I saw sun-creases in the corners of her eyes. She was unembarrassed by our situation.

'Oh, I'm sorry,' I said.

'That's okay. Did you want the bathroom? You went past it. There's one in here, too. You might as well use that now.' She smiled. She pulled on a vest as I walked past her. She smelled of sun lotion. As I closed the door to the en suite, I caught a glimpse of that thong disappearing into the deep cleft of her ass. It was pure magic. I couldn't piss for minutes. I thought I heard Brenna laugh as she shut the bedroom door.

Later, I walked Iris home. She was drunk and woozy and her breath tasted sour when I kissed her. She lay down on her bed. I covered her up in a blanket and went to sleep on the couch.

*

Those few days – less than a week – when we were first together at Iris's seemed elongated, the time stretched and rich in a particular atmosphere that I would never feel again, one that would only be recaptured fleetingly as a sense memory: a sound, a smell, the way the light sometimes falls. It was better because it was temporary; I knew that it needed holding on to in some way. Matthew Trippe's story was swimming in my subconscious too, rising up to surface every few hours and bringing with it a shiver of anticipation, of what it may bring. There was something in me that sought the chaos it promised.

Iris's house had a small raised wooden deck on the back, accessed by opening the first-floor bedroom window and climbing out. The giant palm kept it in shade for much of the day, but for a couple of hours in the morning, the sun threw light and heat through its thick leaves. I pushed the window open and stepped out. I dusted down a small chair and repositioned the tiny metal table so that I could get the typewriter on it. I heard a gate creak open, and as I looked over, Brenna appeared by the neighbour's pool and stood on the flagstones. She pulled her top over her head and took down her skirt. She stood in her underwear. It was plain and white, unfussy. It didn't need to be anything else. She pushed her hair back with both hands and dived in. It was a bad dive. Water divided noisily on either side of her. Brenna swam easily though, lap after lap. The view was kind of deco and painterly, Brenna seen from above, the blue of the water, the white of the concrete, the green of the palms. After a while, she stopped swimming, looked up and saw me. She waved for me to come over.

'Hi,' she said when I got there. 'Pass me the towel.'

There was no ladder but she pushed herself easily from the water and on to the side. I handed her the towel and she wrapped it around herself.

'Hey, Englishman . . . you like watching girls, do you?'

'I do.'

We smiled.

'But it's distracting,' I said. 'I'm trying to work up there.'

'What are you doing?'

'Story for the mag. Some band, you know . . . As always.'

'So,' she said. 'You and Iris . . . Have you yet?'

'Have we what?'

We both smiled again.

'No,' I said. 'Not yet, now that you ask.'

'Ah, that's Iris,' she said.

'What do you mean?'

'Oh nothing . . .' she paused. 'I'm always telling her not to worry about it so much. You met her father though?'

'I did, and Sherry.'

'Iris and her daddy . . .' Brenna said. She unwrapped the towel and began drying her hair with it. 'You know he owns this place, don't you? This place, and ours, and a few others too. He's a lot smarter than he looks, with . . . people like Shelly . . .'

'Sherry.'

'Shelly, Sherry, whoever . . .'

She let it hang there for a moment.

'You . . . and . . . Iris's dad?' I said slowly. Brenna dropped her towel at her feet, picked up her skirt and stepped into it.

'It was all over a long time ago,' she said. 'Iris was a teen-
ager. I knew I'd never last with him, but I loved Iris and she
was all alone with her father. He brought her up, has she told
you that? I was a little too young to mother her and I wouldn't
really say I was the type anyway, but I was a big sister I
suppose . . .'

'And now?'

'And now, Englishman . . . I got fannies to wax . . .'

Brenna pulled on her top, picked up the towel and smirked.
'Come on,' she said. 'I need to lock this place.' We walked back
through the house. I knew there was more but the moment was
passing. Out on the sidewalk, she stopped for a moment. Her
skin was washed in the uninterrupted sunlight.

'This woman I'm doing today has pubes like a carpet,' she
said, and on Fountain the traffic shimmered in the haze.

*

Ray had begun work on the story of Lana, the English singer
who'd moved to LA for the summer, setting up a photoshoot
that we could turn into a road trip as a starting point for the
feature. We'd covered her in the magazine several times before,
and Ray's photographs of her always topped the annual
readers' poll in the 'Sexiest Female' category. Her popularity
was photographic rather than musical, and Lana would come
into the office and take Geoff out for long, boozy lunches
where she'd flirt with him shamelessly and the following
week she'd have a poster of herself in the centre pages, or
the promise of another feature. She was from a town far in the
north of the country, her accent strong and her voice deep;
she was tough and unafraid. I liked her a lot. She had a deal with
an indie label back in England and now she had an apartment

in Marina del Rey, from where she was running her plan to conquer America. Ray wanted us to drive out to the desert and shoot some pictures of Lana and her band there. He invited Iris along too.

As we went to the Marina, I told Iris about Lana. I'd really got to know her when we went on the road in Spain, where she was supporting an ageing and resentful British band called Saxon. We'd begun in Barcelona and then, after an idyllic couple of days spent walking up and down Las Ramblas and going to see the galleon and Gaudi's buildings, we travelled in a tour van driven by a small rat-like man called Juan to Madrid and then high into the mountains to San Sebastian and Bilbao, where Juan's driving had assumed terrifying dimensions. Whenever one of us asked him how much further we had to travel he said 'one hour' and then laughed manically. Several times the van seemed to be about to leave the narrow hairpins and roll off the edge of the mountains over a precipitous drop, and our laughter grew less and less convincing.

When Juan finally made it to the hotel, Lana got out and said to him, 'Juan, you are a fucking bastard,' and Juan had begun to cry. She had been sick for a couple of days by then – while Ray and I and the rest of her band had happily eaten the local food, Lana had insisted on the most 'English' things she could find – and although she went out on stage and pouted provocatively, she ran into the wings on a couple of occasions to throw up into a bucket.

Lana couldn't sing or dance, but she was a beautiful girl and her ambition had not yet been tested. She understood her market perfectly, and she would spend hours after each show posing for photos with shy and ugly teenage boys, kissing their cheeks, ruffling their hair, making them blush and stammer. Some of them made clumsy grabs at her ass or her breasts, or tried to kiss her on the lips. They gave her pieces of paper with poems or drawings on, or asked her to sign magazines and posters, asked her if she had a boyfriend ('Only you, sweetheart,' was her usual reply) or if she remembered them from last time ('I could never forget your face, how are you, love?'). Many had copies of her album, which she would autograph with big kisses. Afterwards she would take a long shower and come back with stories of which of them had terrible halitosis or erupting acne, or which reeked of BO or whose hands had wandered all over her in the crush.

What very few people knew was that Lana was married to her manager, a smart American music industry lawyer called Marty whom she'd met when he threw a party to celebrate a dance single that he'd licensed going to number one in a couple of minor European territories. None of the kids who lined up after her shows would have given a second glance to the expensively dressed, hawk-faced man standing expressionless and silent to one side, nor would they have noticed the looks that sometimes passed between him and Lana. Marty was from a family of monied LA lawyers, but he was trying to carve his own path, away from their influence.

Lana's songs always seemed to feature either gypsies or rainbows or sometimes both. This was down to her brother, Sylvio, who wrote and produced all of them, and played guitar in her band. It's hard to describe him now, in the knowledge of what was to happen, as he was then, but as Iris drove and I talked, I told her about how funny he was, how cocksure and certain about everything, about how the other writers at the magazine laughed at him behind his back and how this absolutely failed to dent his self-image or his confidence; instead he played along in the same way that Lana did, turning preconceptions to their advantage.

I thought we'd be driving all around Marina del Rey using the rather vague directions Marty had given me on the phone, but in the first little side street that Iris turned down stood a silver RV with some kind of aerial on the roof. Ray was leaning against it leisurely smoking a cigarette. He waved as we arrived, and ran around Iris's little red car to open her door. He helped her out, kissed her and squeezed her backside. Iris giggled. Lana walked down the steps of an apartment building opposite, calling out to us and waving. I realised that I hadn't seen her in almost a year. She was tanned, her hair highlighted golden and blonde, her teeth impossibly white. She looked good in the way that Americans looked good, groomed and rich. Her tits had doubled in size. She saw me looking.

'Like 'em do you, love?' she said, and squeezed them together with the tops of her arms. They almost spilled out of her T-shirt. 'All natural, amazing what the sun will do . . .'

I laughed. 'Lana, this is Iris,' I said.

'Hiya, love,' she said, and hugged her too. 'Do you want a look?' she asked, and squeezed them together again. Iris looked.

'Not bad,' she said, and looked again. Lana laughed this time. I felt good. It was going to be alright.

Marty and Sylvio came down the steps together a few moments later. Marty's only concession to the desert was an open-necked shirt under his sports jacket. While Sylvio greeted us – hugging me and Ray, kissing Iris, kissing and hugging Lana whom he had last seen a few moments before – Marty stood slightly apart from us, a fixed smile on his face. He pulled me aside. 'Hey, you can bring your girl, but we're not paying for her.'

'What do you mean, Marty?'

'The hotels . . . food . . . uh, expenses.'

'Are you serious?'

He said nothing.

'Okay, then you just ring all of the other journalists and mags that want to put Lana in, and we'll leave you to it.'

Marty walked off. Ray raised his eyebrows at me. Marty was always trying stuff like that. In his mind, Lana was already a star. Soon we were joined by a couple of others, Tony and Doug, who were Lana's bass player and drummer. They were brothers. Tony had been on the London scene for a while, playing in lots of bands, trying to make it. He had some of their names tattooed on his arms. Doug was just a baby, with his first proper gig. He strutted around like he was in Led Zeppelin. Marty said that there was no room for Tony and Doug in the bus, so they'd have to follow us out to the desert in Tony's car. Tony threw a couple of bags in the back and put his sunglasses on.

We climbed up into the van. Marty got behind the wheel. Sylvio took the bench seat next to him. Iris, Lana and I sat behind. There was plenty of space; Marty just wanted to make it clear that Tony and Doug were hired hands, not part of his big plan.

He manoeuvred the van down the narrow streets of the Marina, the boats moored in long lines, the water calm and sunlit. Through the big back window of the RV we could see Tony and Doug edging along behind us, Tony driving, Doug with his window rolled down and his elbow hanging out, talking to any girl he saw as the traffic edged along. Ray was watching them too.

'Living the dream,' I said. Ray pulled a camera from his bag and started taking pictures of them. Doug checked his hair in the wing mirror. Marty gripped the wheel a little harder. Lana looked up from the magazine she was reading. 'Those fucking two,' she said to no one in particular.

Sylvio put a cassette into the tape deck. It was a Gloria Estefan album that began to play on a permanent loop as we drove away from the ocean and up through the city (it was a record that seemed to be everywhere at the time, and on the rare occasions I hear her voice now it takes me straight back to that trip), and after a couple of hours we were somewhere else, the affluent suburbs giving way to peeling warehouses and storage units, clusters of fast-food outlets and cheap shopping malls, the gaps between them growing bigger, the houses fewer, the sidewalks sliding away into nothing and then just the road and the scrubland beside it, knotted bushes blowing around, the occasional gas station or diner standing in perfect isolation as Marty took us towards the edge of the desert. Tony and Doug kept perfect distance behind us, but as the traffic thinned out and then vanished altogether, the interstate clear for miles in either direction, Tony accelerated and pulled alongside the van. Doug got his torso out of the window and began to try to climb on to the roof while Ray took pictures.

'Oh don't do that,' Iris said softly.

'Don't worry about him, love,' Lana said. 'No fookin' brains. He won't do much damage if he lands on his head.'

Doug slipped back in and Tony accelerated away. The road was so long and straight that it took five minutes for them to disappear from view.

*

They must have driven ten or fifteen miles ahead of us because it took some time for us to catch up, and they were still a mile away when Sylvio pointed down the freeway at what looked like a car pulled over at the side of the highway. The sun glinted from it. As we drew closer, something nearby seemed to be moving.

'For fuck's sake,' said Marty.

Iris, Lana, Ray and I leaned forwards to see what had happened. The car had stopped at an angle, its back end shark-finned on to the freeway and the rest of it in the scrub. Tony and Doug were both lying on the roof, naked except for their shades. As we drew up, Doug began waving his cock around.

Marty pulled the van over in front of them. Lana and Iris were giggling and covering their mouths with their hands. Ray picked up his camera. We jumped out. Marty's face was thunderous.

'Oi oi,' shouted Doug. 'Don't spose any of you lot can fix tyres can you?'

He and Tony slid down from the roof. Doug poked his head back through the open window and pulled out their jeans. They wriggled back into them, the girls pretending not to watch. Ray took some pictures. Sylvio and I walked around to the front of the car. One of the tyres had shredded and the remains of the wheel were sunk in the sand.

'There's no spare,' said Tony, before either of us could ask. 'Took it out so I could fit our gear in.'

'You're fucked then, aren't you,' Sylvio said. 'You'll probably die here. Won't be any other cars along once we've gone.'

'We should try and get it off the road,' I said.

The four of us got behind the trunk and pushed, but it wouldn't move. We tried to shove it sideways by placing our hands on the rear door, but we could only shift it a few inches.

'We'll have to leave it,' Ray said. 'We can probably call someone when we get to Baker. Maybe we can pick it up on the way back.'

'Fuck,' said Marty.

'Got any room in your van, mate?' Tony said to him, but Marty didn't reply. Doug was already throwing their bags into the RV. Iris had wandered a little way from the car and was standing with her back to the road. I walked up behind her and put my arms around her waist. We looked out into the still, flat land that ran all the way to the horizon. I shivered. Something passed through me. She put her hands on mine.

'You okay?' I said.

'Sure.'

The sun was fierce. After a few moments of standing it became oppressive. We climbed into the RV. Tony and Doug joined us in the back. We watched Tony's car through the rear window until it just wasn't there any more.

*

We stopped that night in Baker. The town was nothing more than a few blocks of scorched houses with some bars, a gas station and a couple of motels on the main drag. Beyond the strip were the dark mountains that we would cross the next day. We spent the evening drinking in one of the bars. Marty and Lana had slipped away early. Ray drank in his usual way, steadily and unshakably. It slowed him into his unreachable calm. Sylvio began ordering whiskey and as he got drunker, his stories became more outlandish. Ray and I had heard them on many occasions before, but they had lots of extra flourishes to them. He told Iris about the time he'd jammed with Carlos Santana at the Hammersmith Odeon, an event that as far as Ray and I could tell did happen but that over time had turned from the briefest appearance with another guitarist during a final encore into some kind of jointly headlined show, Carlos and Sylvio trading licks, Carlos finally ceding centre stage to his protégé during one of the all-time great renditions of 'Black Magic Woman'.

'The thing about Carlos,' Sylvio said, 'is that he's very spiritual.' He looked at Iris. 'And I feel that I'm very spiritual too.'

Ray almost spat his drink out. He looked away and fiddled with a cigarette. I choked down a laugh.

'I'm an old soul,' said Sylvio. 'Ray is an old soul too.' He was starting to slur a little, and his eyes were hooded. 'But you . . .' He took Iris's hand. 'You're young, baby. I'm not sure you've been here before . . .' Sylvio's eyes closed, his hands still wrapped around Iris's. I thought he was going to bless her or something, but he became very quiet and I realised he'd gone to sleep. Iris slid her hand from under his, and he finally lifted his head.

'Shall we have brandy and a cigar?' he said.

'I don't think they have them here,' Ray replied.

'I'm for bed then.' Sylvio went around the room kissing us all. He stumbled a little. Iris and I stayed for a while after he'd gone. Tony began talking about Marty. His mood had been bad for days.

'He didn't want us out here,' Tony said. 'But Ray needed the whole band for the pictures.' (Ray was right – because Lana and Sylvio were brother and sister, there was something odd about shooting them together.) 'If we didn't have a tour coming up, I think he might sack us . . .'

'Why's that?' I asked.

'He reckons that Lana has got a thing for Doug.'

I looked over at Doug but he had his head down, staring into his drink. After a while, we finished up and walked back to the motel, where Iris fell asleep right away but I had fractured dreams set out on the road where we had abandoned Tony's car, the landscape still as vast, but now broken up with strangely shaped trees in which great black birds roosted and waited.

★

I was woken by the heat of the sun coming in through the cheap curtains. Iris was stirring too. She rolled over a couple of times. One side of her face had the outline of the pillow seam running down it. She was flushed and tangled in the sheet and when she opened her eyes it seemed to take her a minute to remember where she was. Once she had, she moved quickly around the room. She was deft and light, the way I remembered her at her father's house. She showered, dressed and brushed her hair, and every time she caught my eye, she laughed. She was still self-conscious around me; perhaps she always would be. As I locked the motel door, she hugged me tightly. 'This is fun,' she said.

We walked up main street until we saw a diner. Sylvio, Lana and Marty were already inside. Marty looked up with his hooded eyes.

'Don't worry, Marty,' I said, 'breakfast's on me . . .'

He smiled. I felt for him sometimes. It wasn't easy, following Lana around, knowing what everyone thought of her or how they thought about her. People were hypocrites; well, men were at least. I'd heard some of the things they'd say about Lana and then I'd see them when she was around them, see how she'd made them feel. Most of them could only fantasise about a woman like her. Well, Marty had the reality, not the fantasy, and the reality came with all of this. Sylvio got up and kissed Iris and me good morning. He showed no signs of the night before. He'd pulled his hair back into a ponytail and smelled of various exotic oils. He and Lana both wore sunglasses and they looked oddly similar, despite Lana's American makeover. Breakfast was subdued until Ray arrived. He'd bought a road map at the gas station. He spread it out on the table and began tracing the small thread of roads that cut through the desert and up into the mountains, telling us about a ghost town he'd heard about, and soon the waitress, who was small and blonde and tan and pretty, began directing us along trails that were barely marked on the ridges which signified the great slopes, uninhabited and lunar, that we could see through the window of the diner. The ghost town was called Chloride City and the waitress told us that she'd once driven out there with her high-school friends and they'd camped all night in the mountains, keeping a fire burning and telling one another stories. There was an abandoned mine there too, she said, and the night winds howled eerily from its mouth. She finished talking and cleared away our plates and then came back again with a better map that had the mountain roads clearly marked on it.

Tony and Doug walked through the door and Marty seemed to enjoy telling them that they had arrived too late for breakfast. Chloride City was three hours' drive away easily, maybe more, and then Ray needed to find some locations and get the shoot done while we still had the light. When we were finished with the pictures, we were to drive on to a town called Pahrump for the night, and then circle round on ourselves the next day and head back through Baker and on to LA. Tony glanced at the map and then began asking the waitress about local garages and whether there was anyone who could drive out and tow his car away from the side of the road where we'd left it. She came back to the table again with a pen and a piece of paper and on it she wrote the name and number of a former boyfriend of hers who had a repair and tow business in Bakersfield, which was a few miles further up the interstate.

'I don't know if I want him picking my car up,' Tony said, and when the waitress asked him why, he replied, 'Because if he dumped you, he doesn't know what he's doing.'

Sylvio laughed and Marty raised his eyes to the ceiling, but the waitress giggled and said, 'Oh I broke up with him actually . . . He just wants to fix cars in Bakersfield all his life and well, I don't . . .'

'What do you want to do?' Tony asked her.

'Well, not this,' she said. 'Get out of here, I guess. Maybe I'll go to Vegas. Or LA.'

'We're going back to LA tomorrow,' Tony said. 'Get your ex to fix up my car, and I'll give you a lift . . .'

She laughed. 'Maybe,' she said. 'What do you guys do?'

'We're in a band . . . He's the singer,' Tony said and pointed at Marty.

'Really?' she said, and Doug guffawed, perhaps a little more loudly than he had intended.

'Don't be put off by that mild-mannered exterior,' Tony said.

Marty threw some dollars down on the table and walked out. Iris and I settled the rest and we wandered back towards the motel, the sun in our faces, heat already rising from the road, which shimmered into the distance. Sylvio and Lana followed behind, laughing. Marty was already in the RV when we reached the car park, impassive behind his shades. I went to the room and got our bags and by the time I was back I could see Tony and Doug leaving the diner. Tony crossed the street to use a payphone. Doug took his time, too, and it was some time before Marty started the RV and we left Baker, the Gloria Estefan tape the only thing breaking the noise of the engine and the wheels on the road.

★

We drove for more than an hour before the track started to rise and the landscape changed from the unbroken, heated flatlands of the valley into the sandy, scrub-laden foothills of the mountains, and it took until then for the mood of the morning to lift, which was mostly down to Ray and Iris, who, prompted by Ray, had begun a long and earnest conversation about their sexual histories. It was one of Ray's specialities; he was somehow attuned to the intimacies of the road and the bar and the hotel room and the tour bus, and most of all to the way to talk to women about themselves. Iris was losing her self-consciousness and telling him all about the disastrous affair with the drummer, the move to New York and flight back to LA that ended up at the party where we had met, and then Lana began to join in too, probably to Marty's disapproval, talking about various guys that had come and gone, a couple of them chased off by Sylvio and some inventive threats of violence, and as the girls spoke Ray sat back like a strange kind of zen master, his voice and his laugh carefully modulated to keep the atmosphere, to extend the spell. Iris even took hold of his hand, and while they sat with their fingers inter-locked over the seats, Ray told her how, when he had first met his wife, she hadn't wanted anything to do with him, and how he'd tried everything to get her to go out with him. It was a great story and one which I happened to know was completely untrue, but Iris listened intently, with her eyes opening wider and wider.

'That's so nice,' she said quietly, and then after a moment, 'Too late for me to do that . . .'

Iris and I looked at one another.

'Is it?' I said.

'I think it is,' she replied.

'You're right. We are kind of . . . here, aren't we.'

'Here?'

'On a bus, in the desert, headed for a ghost town. Symbolic . . .'

'Like a novel,' Iris said, her eyes shining.

Ray had pulled out his camera, and took a Polaroid of us at the very moment that Iris stopped speaking. I still have it. Iris has her head tilted towards my shoulder, her crocheted hat slightly askew and one side of her face blurred by the exposure and the bright light of the desert flooding in through the window. At the bottom, where the picture fades into the darkness of the shadows made by the seats, is Ray's thumbprint, created when he'd pulled the Polaroid from the bottom of the camera and fanned it to set the colours.

Marty gunned the RV forwards, beginning to climb more steeply now as we crossed into the mountains proper, the road becoming narrower with drops developing either side of it. Tony had a hold of Ray's map and was twisting it around in his hands, trying to work out where we should leave the highway and take the smaller mountain roads towards the ghost town. Iris sat with her shoulder turned into my chest, my arm across her, the brim of her hat moving gently against the side of my face. Ray gazed out of the window at the sand and rocks and scrubby bushes that lined the mountainsides. A single car passed us, driving quickly down the other side of the road, its driver in shades and two passengers sleeping in the back seat. For a while we took a fork in the road that became narrower and narrower and eventually petered out into a turnaround lined with tyre tracks and beer cans and other detritus that had been thrown from car windows. Doug pleaded with Marty to stop while he took a piss, which Marty did, reluctantly, and Doug pissed in a high fountain into the sand while Tony and Sylvio cheered him on. Tony righted the map, and the RV span around and retraced our path down the track and back on to the mountain. The next fork was the right one, and instead of narrowing as we reached what looked like a canyon edge, it fanned out dramatically, affording us a view of the valley below, in which lay Chloride City, or at least the remains of it; an old wooden hotel with half a roof, four or five dilapidated shacks on either side of it and up above, cut in the side of the hill and almost level with the height of the hotel roof, the mouth of the mine, slim and dark and half blocked by fallen rocks and boulders and wild scrub, its approaches fenced off and lined by warning signs that forbade any approach.

There was no sign of anyone else and no fresh tyre tracks where Marty parked the RV next to a steel water tank that stood at the far end of what passed for the town's street. We got out. The air was thin and warm, the sky a pale and endless blue without a cloud to break it. The view back down the valley was spectacular, a narrow cleft with mountains on either side of it, the steel hulk of a rusting car frame half buried by the sand the only reminder that other human beings had been here. There was a deep and overwhelming silence that had us talking too quickly and laughing too loudly. This was a vast, hot and implacable place, indifferent and unyielding. The sun was already heading west, dropping slowly towards the tops of the mountains, and Ray had perhaps a couple of hours of light left to shoot in. He was getting set up so that the hotel and the street would telescope behind his subject. He banged off a couple of Polaroids; it looked like some kind of film set, almost staged, although everything about it was undoubtedly authentic.

Lana was in the RV with Marty, doing her hair and make-up and changing her clothes. Sylvio, Tony and Doug had taken their stage gear to the old hotel, where they clambered through the half-open door and into the darkness beyond to get ready. Iris slipped her hand into mine.

'Come on,' she said. 'Let them do this. I want to look around.'

We headed back down the valley, past the wrecked car and on towards the shadow cast by one mountain on to the lower slopes of the other. There was something about the perspectives of this place that skewed distance. We walked for a while longer, Iris's hand hot in mine, and when we turned around to look back, the ghost town was tiny, the figures of Ray and Lana and the band like stick figures. Eventually we reached the shade of the upslopes and their deep and welcoming cool. Iris stopped and looked around. She stood in front of me.

'Don't say anything,' she said. She took off the crocheted hat and pulled her top over her head. She unclasped her bra, took off her shoes and wriggled out of her jeans. She hooked her fingers into her panties and slid them off too.

'Now you,' she said.

My hands shook as I did. I knew what this meant. I bent down and picked up her hat. I put it back on her head. She smiled; she looked incredible, a pale and gentle thing against the harsh dirt.

'Now?' I said.

'Mmm hmmm,' she said softly. 'Now.'

Afterwards we lay together on our clothes. The silence around us was total.

'Why?' I asked her after a while. 'Why today?'

'I don't know,' she said. 'It'll be alright now, though . . .'

'Will it?'

'Oh yes,' she said. 'Yes it will. It's just hard for me the first time. I can't say why. It's always been that way.'

I looked at Iris. She still had the hat on. She touched a place in me that no one else had. We fucked again, more intimately, and when it was over, looked up to see that the hills had darkened considerably and the sun was almost down. We dressed quickly, completely at ease with one another now.

'This *is* like a novel, isn't it,' she said.

'A cool one, Iris. Not the sort of book I usually get to read . . .'

'Well, maybe you will from now on,' she said.

We began to walk back towards Chloride City. As we got closer, the others came back into view. Ray was shooting into the setting sun now, doing some individuals of Lana. Marty stood next to Ray, the hunch to his shoulders slight but unmistakable. The others had climbed up to the mine entrance and were looking down across the valley. I wondered if we would seem any different to them. There was a lightness between Iris and me that hadn't been there before, or at least that was how it felt to me. We scrabbled up the edge of the rocky slope to where Sylvio, Tony and Doug were standing.

'Where have you two been?' asked Sylvio.

I was about to reply when Iris said, 'Oh, he's been down a mineshaft.'

*

By the time we'd packed up the RV, the sun was down behind the mountain, and an eerie, quiet dusk had settled. Marty had to drive slowly back up the track, the edges of the road less distinct in the disappearing light. The engine laboured as he kept shifting gears to cope with the climb. We came to the fork in the road, and Marty, Sylvio and Lana had a brief argument over which way we should go, Lana siding with Sylvio, but Marty ignored them and took the fork he wanted, and when we got back to the broader, more solid road that led to the highway, he smirked. Lana dug him in the ribs.

'You love to be fookin' right, don't you . . .' she said, but then she put her arm across his shoulders and laid her head down next to his. Marty actually seemed happy. He drove determinedly on to Pahrump while a torpor set on the rest of us as the last of the day slipped away and the blackness of the desert filled the windows. Soon everyone was asleep. I leaned over to the front to chat to Marty, just to make sure that he was finding the driving okay. 'Look,' he said, and he pointed as the headlights caught the glowing white eyes of a small pack of coyotes that were pulling and tugging at the carcass of some roadkill. They scattered as we got closer, the tail of the last one to leave just scooting out of the way as we passed.

It took another two hours to reach Pahrump. We checked into the Nugget Casino and went straight to the bar, where we sat among the chirruping slot machines and in the zinging light, a place that couldn't have been more different to where we had spent the day. For some reason everyone was drinking quickly, not saying much, and I drifted into a brief reverie, imagining this place in 200 years' time as a ghost town of its own, the casino a vast wreck open to the stars, the hulks of slot machines and poker tables half buried by sand and people travelling for miles to stand in it and feel its weird desolation. Iris drank three beers and fell asleep for a few moments; when she woke, she put her hand on the top of my head, picked up the key to her room and disappeared towards it. Sylvio and Tony were drunkenly telling one another what great musicians they were. Lana and Doug huddled together at a table on their own, Doug talking quite animatedly and Lana laughing and looking coyly at him, laughing loudly and often. She picked up a beer bottle and pretended to stroke it like a cock. Suddenly I was aware of Marty's face close to mine.

'Look at that . . .' he said in a low, slightly menacing voice. 'Look at them. That's what I'm talking about. That's what I'm *saying* . . .'

'C'mon, Marty, they're hammered,' I said. 'And so are you. All day in the sun and then beer.'

He laughed, somewhat bitterly. 'You . . .' he said. 'You have no idea.'

'No idea about what, Marty?'

He laughed again, a little more loudly. 'Think I'm going to tell you?' He drained his beer and signalled the waitress for another. He began a long and rambling speech full of non-sequiturs about how many years he'd spent qualifying as a lawyer and how he wanted to make his father proud of him so he'd set out to find an artist of his own that he could turn into something just as his father had done, but he'd been sidetracked by meeting Lana and he'd become involved in her ambitions and dreams and fallen in love and now they were here. 'It's like I say to her,' he slurred, 'I can do all of this' – he swung his arm around, almost knocking his beer bottle from the table – 'I can do all of this, but I can't sing the fucking songs, can I? No one wants to see my fucking tits, do they . . .' He glared across at Lana and Doug, who were still lost in their conversation. 'You can get used to a lot of things . . . a lot of things . . . but you can't get used to every man that comes into the store wanting to fuck your wife . . . no one gets used to that in a hurry, that's for sure.'

He stopped for a moment. 'Anyway, that shit's not what I'm talking about. Him . . .' He pointed at Doug, not very subtly. 'He's the one . . . He's the one . . . I see what he's doing . . .'

Marty looked directly at me, although he was so drunk he couldn't quite stop his head from swaying gently from side to side. 'But don't worry . . . I know something about him. She doesn't think it's true but it is . . . She'll find out.' He smiled again, this time to himself, got unsteadily to his feet and began to make his way through the casino. I watched him as he weaved through the tables and into the shadows. I still had most of a beer left so I sat and let the casino's strange torpor settle over me, watching the people lolling in front of the slots and the waitresses cruising between the tables, thinking about Marty and what he could possibly know about Doug and it was a shock when he appeared back at my side from out of nowhere and sat down heavily in the seat next to me, a fresh beer in his hand, his hooded eyes almost black and impossible to read as he moved his face closer to mine.

'I was watching the desert today,' he said. 'While I was driving I was looking out there at all that space. No one knows what's out there, man, not me, not you, not anyone . . . When my dad was with Sinatra, they used to come out here . . . He knows some things . . .' Marty smiled the thin smile again. I was pretty sure he was full of shit and also he was too drunk to really make much sense, but he was right, it was easy to stare out into the desert and get spooked by what might have happened in its affectless reaches.

'Each man finds what he's looking for in the desert,' Marty said.

'What does that mean?' I asked him.

'Maybe you'll see. Maybe you'll all find out . . .'

Marty got up and left again, but this time he walked purposefully through the casino and towards the lifts and he didn't seem half as drunk as he had a few minutes before. I gave an involuntary shiver and then smiled at how stupid that was.

Soon afterwards, Lana and Doug got up to leave too and after Doug had got out of the lift at his floor – with nothing more than a friendly wave for Lana, I noticed – she said to me, 'So what were you and my drunk husband talking about? More of his paranoia?'

'No,' I said. 'He was okay. You should just give him a break . . .'

'Never,' she said, and kissed me on the cheek. She took her key from her bag. 'He does alright, doesn't he . . . He gets me . . .'

I watched her disappear down the corridor while I dug out my own key from my pocket and fumbled it into the lock. The night light was still on and Iris was lying face down on the bed, half in its glow. She'd started to undress but seemed to have fallen asleep halfway through, one leg still in her jeans. I got up on to the bed next to her and after a few minutes she must have realised I was there as she stirred, resting her head on my chest and wiping her mouth on her wrist. 'Hey,' she said, her voice croaky with sleep, her eyes too heavy to open fully. 'Don't do that, will you?'

'Do what?' I asked.

'What they all do,' she said and then closed her eyes again. I thought that she was dreaming, but then she looked at me again and said, 'They all do that.'

*

When we left Pahrump, the streets were empty and the sun reflected so hard from them you had to wear shades to kill the glare. We were soon clear of town and back out on the desert highway where we drove for a couple of hours in near-silence, people either still sleeping or immobilised by their hangovers. I stared out of the window, thinking every now and again of Marty, who drove with his usual absorption. I wondered what he was thinking of as he watched the road, whether he remembered what he had said to me in the casino bar. That morning, Iris had woken early and taken a long shower and as she dried herself and dressed, I told her what Marty had said. 'Everyone who grows up in LA has stories like that,' Iris replied. 'People who disappear in the desert. My father says that some guy he knew who was in debt was supposed to have been found without his hands or his feet. When I was in high school there was this video that went around and it was supposed to be a real-life snuff movie. It was this girl in a car, she was kind of drugged or something, there were these couple of guys were driving her out beyond Palm Springs at night-time, and when they stopped the car they kind of threw her out and beat her up a bit and then they left her there, just turned the car around and drove off real fast, but then the cops came around to the school and said they knew we'd been passing it around and it was definitely a fake. A lot of it's horse shit. People from LA disappear all the time.'

In Baker, we went for lunch back in the diner and the blonde waitress told Tony that his car was fixed up and ready at the garage just out of town and when Tony asked her if she still wanted to come to LA with him, she just laughed and shrugged and walked away. Marty drove to Bakersfield and Doug loaded their stuff into Tony's car while Tony handed over a couple of hundred dollars that he'd had to borrow from Marty as an advance. Marty didn't bother waiting for them; instead he got into the RV and drove fast all the way back to LA.

★

Later there was a record company party for some band or other at the Mondrian that Ray had got us all into. Iris and I went to the Hyatt rather than to her house on Fountain – she was quite insistent about it – and after I'd picked up my messages, which were essentially all from the magazine giving me various deadlines and other stories to set up plus one rambling, almost nonsensical transcription by the receptionist of a conversation she'd had with someone called 'Ronnie', we went to bed and then to the rooftop pool where we stood by the rail nursing beers and watched the traffic on Sunset move in its hypnotic, lulling way, Iris looking hot in a short skirt, my mind drifting to the underwear I'd watched her slide into and wondering what was going to happen between us. People splashed in the pool even though the wind was starting to pick up and Iris's bare skin was puckered in the cool. I stood behind her and wrapped her in my arms. She leaned her head backwards towards mine. Ray showed up and he and Iris each sneaked a cigarette. 'Good time in the desert?' he said, and Iris laughed and whispered something in his ear. Soon Sylvio appeared wearing his usual cutaway T-shirt and smelling of patchouli and we stayed on the roof until the sun dipped into the distant sea and the wind chilled the air and then took the lift down to the bar where the same sad-voiced woman from a few nights ago was singing and the free buffet was out and the only other people in there were a couple of exhausted-looking businessmen in crumpled suits.

'Is Lana coming tonight?' Iris asked Sylvio.

'Yeah, if she can leave Marty,' he said. 'He had some kind of freak-out after we got back.'

'What about?'

'I dunno, love. He's a crazy dude, as they say.'

We stayed in the bar for a while longer and then walked

over to the Mondrian, the wind still stirring the palms and blowing at Iris's skirt, which she held down with one hand. The party was on the roof at the Skybar, where they had lit the pool from underneath and placed Klieg lights at various places on the floor that were throwing coloured beams up on to the night clouds, reflecting off them as they sailed overhead, the high glass walls sheltering everyone from the winds. We had arrived early and the place was almost empty and the DJ was already playing Mötley Crüe and the Ratt and Poison, LA Guns and Faster Pussycat, music that seemed at odds with the expensive, low-key decadence of the surroundings, but as the lifts began to bring more and more people up, the bar began to fill and young and good-looking waitresses and waiters, nearly all of them blonde and tanned, came out with trays of hors d'oeuvres and shots of mescal and the atmosphere changed.

I watched Iris sneak a mescal. She was talking to some guys from some low-level band or other – easy to pick once you'd seen enough of them; they looked, superficially, like the guys in bands who had record deals and were playing shows and appearing in magazines, except their clothes were too cheap, their make-up too artlessly applied, their pleasure at being here too apparent, their laughter too loud. They kept leaning close to Iris, talking into her ear, competing for her attention. After a while she looked over and caught my eye and smiled. I smiled back, and watched her for a minute, listening to the DJ, who was now playing Great White, Warrant and Jane's Addiction. I saw Sylvio, who beckoned me over. He was talking to a couple of girls whom I didn't know, one blonde and one dark, both giggling at what he was saying, and he introduced me, dropping the name of the magazine right away, and the dark girl said, 'Ooh, I heard Iron Maiden is coming tonight.'

'Let's hope so,' said Sylvio, and I had to stifle a guffaw, and after a while the girls drifted off and Sylvio and I went to the bar where I saw Alan Niven, an English guy who managed Great White and wrote most of their songs and who was now managing Guns N' Roses too, and he slipped me a couple of tickets to the VIP room, which wasn't really a room but instead a sectioned-off quarter of the bar separated by a little rope and with a bouncer standing by it. There was barely anyone inside, just Kevin DuBrow, who sung with Quiet Riot, sitting in silence with his girlfriend, both looking bored, and a few record company people talking more animatedly and a ridiculously beautiful girl who was sitting alone in one corner and nodding her head gently to the music.

The night was frictionless and long, as calm as the opulent surroundings which seemed to deaden the effects of the vast amounts of cocaine that were being taken less than discreetly in the bathrooms, the queues stretching out of the cloakroom and back into the bar itself, people walking out rubbing at their noses and gums, glassy and wired and animated now. A girl called Blair who I knew vaguely from somewhere came over and draped around my neck one of the thin scarves she was wearing, pulling on it and asking if I wanted to dance, which I didn't, so instead she said, 'Hey, want to bump a line with me?' and when I told her I didn't dance or take drugs or enjoy myself in any way, she laughed and asked if I'd mind lining up with her in the queue for the restroom anyway. I said okay, and as it inched towards the doors, she told me about her father, who was in the movie business and who gave her a large allowance and who had unwittingly introduced her to his cocaine dealer, Mark, who was now supplying both of them and with whom she'd been having a casual kind of fling that she'd somehow drifted into. 'When I'm high,' she said, 'I find him very arousing,' and then she giggled and said, 'even though he's got to be, like, thirty-five or something, which like, you know . . . gross, usually . . .' she laughed again, 'but he's sort of one of the best dealers in West Hollywood because his coke's really good and I know for a fact that Eddie Van Halen buys from him because I saw them together once at the Roxy, and Eddie was pretty far gone, it was like, really *obvious*, and Mark's best stuff, it fucking knocks you on your ass, I mean, I thought I was OD-ing once because I was seeing these, like, lights in my eyes even though my friend said that my eyes had actually, like, rolled back in my head, and then I got this really heavy nosebleed right afterwards so I had to kind of stop for a little while, but you know . . .' She paused for a second to put her hand in the pocket of her jeans and pulled out a little baggie, which she waved at me. 'I'm ba-aaack . . .'

I glanced around anxiously. Drugs of any sort always put me on edge, but no one was paying any attention to us, instead they were wrapped up in their own thing, and anyway, the DJ had cranked up a couple of notches and it was pretty hard to make out anything anyone was saying unless they were standing with their face practically in yours, which I noticed then that Blair was.

'Am I talking too much?' she asked, 'because it's like, one of my bad habits . . .' We reached the restroom. 'Sure you don't want a bump?' she said, waving the baggie again and giggling. 'Mark's finest . . .' She ducked inside the cubicle with a little wave and when she came back out again, she smiled wickedly and took my hand. 'That was good,' she said. 'Really, like, *bang*, you know . . . Hey shall we get a drink?' and without waiting for me to answer, Blair plunged through the crowd towards the bar where she threw down a couple of shots of mescal and took a beer. 'Ooh, fiery throat,' she said croakily, and stumbled a little as we moved over towards the pool, where she almost walked into Iris.

'Oh, hey Iris,' Blair said, and as they hugged, Iris looked over Blair's shoulder and gave me a quizzical look.

'Hey! You two know each other?' Blair asked, sounding genuinely surprised.

'Oh yes,' Iris smiled, and gave me a little kiss.

'Ooh . . . how cool,' said Blair. 'You want to come back to my house? I'm like, not really feeling it here tonight.'

★

I woke up the next morning on a giant leather sofa in a chill and shaded room, a blade of light from a gap in the drapes falling on my face. I looked around and saw Iris curled up at the other end, and Blair asleep in a giant recliner across the room, various bits of clothing scattered on the floor and a giant television flickering silently between us. I walked through the deserted mansion looking for a bathroom (the one I found was the same size as my hotel room, marbled and sleek and immaculately clean) where I took a long shower while I thought about the events of last night – Blair calling her driver from the courtesy phone at the Skybar, having to yell into the receiver above the din of the band that had turned up to play (the party was actually for them, but they arrived so late the mood had tipped from languor to indifference); the three of us sitting in the cool dark of the limo, the windblown palms at the roadsides looming tall and black through the tinted windows; Blair offering her father's cognac, which was secreted in a coldbox under one of the seats; Iris and Blair explaining to me how they had met, at the all-girls high school that they had both attended, a private college of choice for LA's monied, distracted parents; the car taking the freeway exit and then gliding through a maze of gated streets before drawing up in the driveway of a simply vast house with a colonnaded entrance so large that it towered over the two pretty big palms that stood on either side of it, Blair giggling as she tried to remember the code that turned off the alarms and electronically slid back the deadlocks; the original art, including a Picasso sketch, that hung on the walls; Blair leading us through room after room until we came to the open-plan living area I'd woken up in, with its luxurious bespoke furniture and giant Japanese television in a cabinet that matched the floor-to-ceiling shelves filled with video tapes; Blair picking a movie and then pulling the baggie from her jeans and racking out more lines on an oak coffee table, snorting a couple back with practised ease and rubbing the debris into her gums; Iris and Blair getting up and dancing together when a song they liked came on the soundtrack of the movie that was playing (Blair's father's latest, apparently, a convoluted story about a group of college kids going home for Christmas, almost every scene cut like a video and scored with knowing electro-pop); Iris falling asleep before the movie was over, Blair doing more coke and then sliding up next to me and saying, 'Hey, so, shall we go put on a porno upstairs and jerk off together?' and me amazing myself by turning her down (she looked great in a simple white vest, her hand sneaking into the top of her jeans, exposing her flat, tan stomach), something that now, as the comforting warmth of the shower enveloped me, had me realising that Iris had taken a hold on my life.

I towelled off and dressed and walked back through the house, wandering into the kitchen by mistake. A smiling and silent maid, in uniform, steered me back towards the living room, where Blair was snoring quite loudly and Iris was propped up at one end of the sofa, her feet pulled up under her, shoes already on. 'Hey,' she said, standing up, 'let's go,' and without waiting for me she began making her way towards the front door.

We stepped outside on to the cool of the shaded driveway and made our way down to the gate, where Iris had the maid buzz us through. Everything was still and hushed, no traffic, no movement from behind the gates of the similarly vast houses set behind their high walls.

'Do you know where we are?' I asked Iris.

'The Palisades somewhere. We came along Sunset but I wasn't really looking. I just wanted to get out of there. I've got to stop drinking so much . . . I don't even like Blair, I can't believe we came back here.'

I put my arm around her. She seemed sad and it gave me a sudden feeling of uncertainty. We walked for a while in silence, the streets widening, the traffic noise rising, the breeze picking up as we got nearer to the ocean. In a run of shops near the Pacific Coast Highway we found a place to have breakfast, where Iris ate hungrily, her hangover clearing, her mood levelling, and we began talking properly for the first time since we left Chloride City, which already seemed weeks ago in the strange, accelerated time we were living. Iris told me how shocked she'd been to see me with Blair at the party, a collision of worlds because she hadn't seen Blair for some years but when they'd been at school she'd been the richest kid there, the centre of a hip, bitchy and druggy circle that lived hedonistic lives lacking in any apparent ambition, spending their free time drifting through shopping malls and each other's vast houses, the group shifting subtly but constantly as people fell in and out of favour with Blair; a girl she mocked for her looks becoming lost in a hell of anorexia and self-loathing, another refusing to eat until her parents consented to a breast augmentation, more dark rumours that Blair had been videotaped having a threesome with a couple of hot young actors, one of whom 'punches her in the face at the conclusion of the tape because she can't make him come', the tape discovered when a copy was passed to Blair's father by one of his assistants who'd been watching it with his girlfriend, the young actor hastily dropped by his agent and last seen making porn movies somewhere in the Valley.

Iris barely moved as she spoke, the words coming quickly in one long sentence as the memories almost overwhelmed her. We ordered more coffee and juice and she began again, a story about herself at another party, this one attended by Blair's brother and his friends, a couple of years older and back from college, one of whom spent the night drinking with Iris, both becoming drunker and drunker and inevitably ending up together in one of the bedrooms where they'd stripped off and Iris had gone down on him for a long time without making him hard, him getting more and more irritated with what he called her 'lack of technique' even though he was so drunk by that point he could barely talk. He'd given her 'some sort of drink' that was sweet and sticky and had made her feel cold and almost impossibly tired. She had fallen asleep, the boy still with her, holding her, and by the time Iris woke, the party was done and everyone had left.

Soon afterwards, Iris had gone on vacation with her father and while she was away had missed her period. After more weeks of worry she had confided in Brenna who had taken her to her doctor, who confirmed that Iris was pregnant. The days that followed were the worst of her life – her voice would have betrayed that truth had she not been so willing to speak it, it was high and almost cracking with sadness now – as she came to the realisation that the boy, or maybe boys, had fucked her while she was intoxicated or asleep or whatever she'd been. She decided to go ahead with an abortion, which was done at a clinic in San Diego, Brenna telling her father that they were away for 'a girls' weekend'.

By the time she had finished telling me all of this, large tears were rolling down her face and falling on to the table, her hand gripping mine so tightly that the knuckle of her thumb had turned white.

'Aah sorry,' she said, wiping her face with her hand and ignoring the napkin I'd pulled from the dispenser for her. 'I hate that it still upsets me but it all makes me so fucking angry.'

'Why didn't you say something last night? I feel terrible, Iris.'

'You couldn't know. And it's not her fault, although she is fucked up and not someone I like, but I kind of feel sorry for her too.'

'What if her brother had been there?'

'That's unlikely. He died in a car wreck in Laurel Canyon a couple of years ago. He was driving at night, lost it on the bends. The car got buried in these bushes, so it took them a few days to find him. It was in all the papers. There was some rumour that it wasn't an accident because everyone knew he was dealing, but you know, this is LA . . . no one dies without a rumour . . .'

She gave me a thin smile. She looked slightly better now. I wondered whether to tell her about Blair and the jerking-off thing from last night. I decided I would, and when I did, her eyes glistened with more tears.

'That would be nothing for her,' she said. 'Did you want to?'

'No,' I said. 'No I didn't . . . I'm not that kind of guy.'

It was a weak joke, but Iris smiled anyway.

'All guys are that type of guy,' she said.

'I think you might be right. But just not last night.'

'That's good. Let's try and make this last for a while, shall we? I'm having a nice time . . .'

'Me too,' I said. 'Me too . . .'

We settled up and walked down to the highway where we found a payphone and Iris rang for a car on her office account, and while we waited for it to come she bought some cigarettes and smoked two or three in a row, lighting one from the other and pulling the smoke deep into her lungs.

'I don't do this very often, either,' she said, raising her cigarette, 'but I guess you're finding out all sorts of things about me.'

The car arrived and took us back through the silent Palisades, past the giant houses in their sleepy sadness and up on to Sunset where the morning traffic was slow and we sat in the heat haze until Iris leaned forward to the driver and said, 'Take Fountain.'

5. The Impressionist

The car took us back to Iris's, but she was washed out and edgy and raw and she didn't want to stay for whatever reason, so she packed a small bag and we went to the Hyatt, where Iris used one of her father's business cards to upgrade the room to a large suite on a private floor and a view over Sunset.

The suite was ours for a week. Iris said that her father used so many hotels he received free upgrades all the time. She fussed around unpacking her bag. She seemed much happier here. She said that the two girls who shared the house with her and Brenna had given notice and were moving out to a place in Brentwood and she didn't want to be around with all of the upheaval as they left. She had also called her office and taken the rest of the week off. She said she was going to 'assist' me instead. I read through the messages I'd picked up before the party. I called the number, which had an LA area code, on the receptionist's garbled note from 'Ronnie' and when someone finally answered, it turned out to be Donald who without any preamble and in a voice deep with irritation began telling me about the latest in the case of Matthew Trippe.

'Listen, man,' he said, sounding vaguely ridiculous, 'you can't give anyone this number. I've rented an office out here in LA for a while. I'm gonna give you the address. You've gotta get out here, okay. Now, you got a pen?'

Donald gave me an address somewhere in the Valley and pedantically asked me to read it back to him. He then began a lengthy description of how to find the place, what it looked like and where to park, and then he told me how difficult it had been for him to rent, how much it was costing him, what an asshole the owner was. He went on and on.

'Anyway,' he said at last, 'the lawsuit is ready, man. It's going to be filed with the court today. I want you to come and read it. It's real strong now and it's gonna blow your fucking mind. I mean, this shit's unreal that they've got away with here. Come out tomorrow at six, and I guarantee you, man, you'll have your story. I've got a big surprise for you. Don't be late, man. Six o'clock . . .'

That night, Iris and I took a drive out to the Pacific Coast Highway and headed a few miles up the coast. We stopped at one of the inlets and stood on the rocks above the beach as the wind blew in and the breakers crashed on the shore. In the distance we could see the lights of Catalina, shining across the dark sea. We walked a little way and found a beach shack that had been turned into a little restaurant that served seafood, with barely anyone in it. We took a table out on the deck and sat in rickety chairs drinking Diet Coke and eating delicious fresh fish straight from the chef's galley. Iris did some deadpan impressions of Donald; she was an excellent mimic. She had him down pat, his Southern drawl, his affected manner, his ludicrous hippy turn of phrase. Then she did Marty, too, reproducing his mirthless laugh and his unblinking stare. I laughed. It was good to see her spirit returning. Iris was damaged, but she was a fighter. We sat out there by the ocean until the wind got stiff and cold, and then we drove back to the Hyatt, our route taking us through the Palisades and, I realised, past Blair's house, the lights off, the gates shut, everything apparently empty. Iris stared over for a moment, but said nothing more about it.

*

We woke late. Iris had offered me her car for the trip out to the Valley. She spent part of the afternoon drawing me a map of how to find Donald's office; it was precise and detailed, with little landmarks picked out and described in her neat, tiny hand. She thought it would take an hour or so in the evening traffic, and I left myself an extra half an hour in case I got lost. Donald seemed like he was on the verge of losing it in everyday conversation, and I didn't want to have to listen to his bullshit if he felt any more put upon than he had to be.

The evening was cool and still and I had taken the top down on the little red car. I took Mulholland up into the hills, the radio on, the traffic light. I realised how rarely I was alone here. For the first time in a while I felt foreign and out of place. I tried to shake it off by turning up the radio and driving a little faster, but I'd always found that the hills had an odd atmosphere. They could be alien and unsettling. Who knew what was in the canyons that gaped beyond the roadsides, or the hillsides that dropped away steeply from the tight bends? I thought of Blair's brother, dead in his car, concealed by the trees and bushes. It wasn't until I crossed the top of Laurel Canyon and began to descend towards the Valley that the slight feeling of doom lifted and I smiled at myself for entertaining it. Maybe it was Donald and his weird stories of Matthew Trippe. I wondered what new dimensions the story had taken on. The files that he'd given me were compelling in their way, but circumstantial too, dependent on the credibility of his only witness. I tried not to consider what I was getting into, but as I came down the canyon edge, the DJ played Mötley Crüe. Donald's voodoo was working.

Just as Iris had said, the traffic in the Valley began to thicken up. I drove through Studio City and took the Ventura Freeway towards Sherman Oaks, crawling along from stop light to stop light now, each beginning to get brighter in the gathering dusk. As Iris had drawn on her map, I went past La Reina theatre and the National Bank tower and took a right on to the San Diego Freeway, the easy affluence of Sherman Oaks giving way to the low-rise flatlands of Van Nuys, blocky units and tract houses lining the roads, the sidewalks of the streets not the sun-bleached broadways of a rich town but the cracked and uncared-for pathways of LA's overlooked interior, the buildings on each corner tagged with graffiti, the cars that purred through the canyons and hills now older, noisier models. I drove for a while and then slipped from the freeway on to Sepulveda Boulevard and then into the little grid of streets that Donald had described, taking a couple of wrong turns before I arrived in front of a row of glass-fronted offices on short-term lets, about half of them with real-estate agents' boards, a couple of those offering daily and even hourly rates. I parked up and checked the time. I was half an hour early. I walked back to the row of offices and peered in some of the windows. A couple had piles of unopened mail on the floor just inside the door, another had a bored-looking girl sitting behind a desk who stood up and smoothed down her skirt before slumping back in her chair again as I passed. Donald's unit was towards the far end. I decided not to go straight in; instead I crossed the road where there was a coffee shop with some sun-stained parasols guarding the plastic chairs out on the kerbside. I found one towards the back and sat in the deep shade, pretty sure I would be invisible to anyone looking across from the offices opposite. I had a good view of Donald's unit, which had a venetian blind pulled halfway down the window. The last of the sun was glinting from the glass as it set, so it probably spent most of the day swinging around directly into the offices. No wonder they were cheap and half-empty. I sipped on an iced tea and watched. The bored-looking girl came out and locked up her office door, checking her reflection in the glass before pulling a pair of sunglasses from her shoulder bag, setting them carefully on her face and walking briskly down the street without a backwards glance. There was no movement at all from Donald's office and I wondered whether he was actually there; there was something about the stillness that suggested he wasn't but at five to six the door jerked open and he stepped out on to the kerbside, looking one way down the street and then the other, and then glaring at his watch. His hair was bunched in a straggly ponytail, and he had an old baseball hat pulled down over his eyes. I drained my tea, got up and waved over towards him at which point he stood bolt upright and beckoned furiously.

'Hey, man, come on over, come on,' he said quite loudly, and before I was halfway across the road he had dived back inside, the door shuddering behind him, and when I got there he was already back behind his desk, a ceiling fan effortlessly stirring the warm air, which bore a faint smell of mildew.

'Nice place you've got here,' I said, a comment Donald ignored; instead he scrabbled around in a pile of papers by his feet and pulled out a copy of the lawsuit that he had filed on behalf of Matthew Trippe.

'Okay,' he said, 'I'm gonna leave you to read this. I'll go get us coffee.'

Donald disappeared through the door before I could tell him that I didn't drink it.

I settled back in the chair and began to read. The little I knew about American lawsuits I had learned from Iris's father during the weekend at his house. He had explained that they should be as aggressive as possible and cover every aspect of the complaint, however small. It was hard to think of anything that better suited Donald's nature. He was a tenacious guy, weird and excluded by most of the world but nonetheless not the kind of person who could be disregarded. He was easily underestimated. I wondered if it was a mistake that Doc McGhee would make.

I began to read, leafing through the first few pages, which set out the parts of the story that I already knew. I imagined myself in the position of a judge or someone hearing the arguments for the first time, a person unfamiliar with the world that the pages described. The names of the protagonists, instead of appearing famous and unapproachable, would look cartoonish and odd, the music they made a generic approximation of everything else that played on MTV and rock radio, their achievements temporary and soon replaced by the next big fad. Doc, a figure of such authority and wealth, was a hustler who had narrowly avoided jail and had somehow gotten lucky with another of his scams. Would a man that smuggled 29,000 lb of marijuana through North Carolina be capable of switching around a couple of kids in face paint to play a rock 'n' roll show? Was the character of 'Nikki Sixx' a construct that could be represented by different people at different times? Was Matthew Trippe exactly the kind of biddable, borderline dumb kid who could be exploited in order to keep the money coming in? Were Mötley Crüe aware enough of the fleeting nature of chance, and the need to seize it when it came?

Cast in that light, the case became something else, something plausible or at least something arguable. Donald clattered back in through the door, breaking my line of thought. He was holding two cups of coffee, one of which he set heavily on the desk in front of me, some of the froth spilling from the edges of the lid.

'Drink that quickly,' he said. 'We've gotta go.'

'Go where, Donald?'

'I told you man, I got a surprise for you. It's gonna blow your fucking socks off. Now, what do you think of that, buddy?' He pointed to the lawsuit.

'Well I only—'

'It's *astonishing*, isn't it,' he said, still in his own world and talking across me, 'the bullshit they think they can get away with. I tell you, they ain't getting away with this. I mean the facts that we establish in there are *overwhelming*, aren't they? Beyond any doubt they are. Now, you got your car, man?'

'Sure, it's just across the street.'

'Okay, well mine is too. It's the black truck there. You follow me, okay? And stick tight, man.'

'Where are we going?'

'You'll see. You're going to get your story. Now let's get going, come on . . .'

Donald's truck looked as old as everything else he had. The tailgate was hanging open on one side and mud was sprayed all over the paintwork. He turned into the traffic on Sepulveda and I tucked in behind him. We headed back to the interstate and went north. Donald drove quickly, impatiently changing lanes, usually without signalling. We took an exit beyond Granada Hills and pulled up in the car park of a small plaza ringed with fast-food places, bars and late-night stores. I parked next to Donald. He jumped down from his cab and walked quickly into one of the bars, where he bought a couple of beers and slid one towards me. We drank for a while. It was so loud in there I couldn't really hear what he was saying so I just nodded and smiled in the right places and studied his face, which had a sense of almost permanent disappointment to it, downcast and lined; when he did laugh it had an undercurrent of bitterness rather than humour. While he talked on, I remembered a little more of what Iris's father had said about suing people in America. He had a couple of lawsuits of his own going on – he found it hard it remember a time when he didn't. It was just another way of doing business, he said. If the parties were roughly equivalent in size, it was a method of dispute resolution, a way of bringing someone to the table and forcing a solution through. Where one party was big and the other was small, it was something different; often it was easier and cheaper for the larger party to settle quietly. 'Just make it go away,' he had said. 'Doesn't really matter if it's wrong or right – you're not admitting anything by paying up. What you're doing is saving yourself the aggravation of carrying on. Some lawyers make a good living doing that.'

I wondered how Iris's father would deal with Donald. It struck me that a minor settlement would be the worst outcome for Donald, because he didn't want this to go away, he wanted it to carry on. It would almost be better for him if he lost – if that happened he would simply become more obsessive about it, more embittered and recalcitrant, even more of a pain in the ass. He would go on for ever. I wasn't sure yet what Donald did want but I was pretty sure of what he didn't. He wasn't after a few thousand dollars of Doc's, handed over for a quiet life. This was something a lot more personal, not even really to do with Matthew or Mötley Crüe.

I sipped the beer that Donald had given me, while he threw them back, finishing three or four bottles.

'Okay,' he said suddenly. 'It's time. Let's go, man.'

We walked outside. Donald looked out across the parking lot. The section that was furthest away from the plaza was almost deserted and Donald headed directly towards it, barely waiting for me to keep pace. The noise of the bars quickly died away. In the far corner of the lot was a single parked car and as we drew closer to it, it flashed its headlights at us.

'This is it, man,' said Donald. 'You ready?' He waved wildly at the car, gesturing for whoever was inside to get out. He'd evidently planned this little flourish quite carefully: it was like a bad B-movie, accentuated by the film noir setting, the dark car, the empty lot, this bare patch of ground illuminated by the monochrome flare of the street lights.

The door opened and Matthew Trippe stepped out, or rather, Nikki Sixx did, the version from the videos and the pages of the magazines, the jet-black hair in a towering back-comb, full stage make-up with a streak of war paint beneath each eye (something 'Nikki Sixx' had now stopped doing but certainly the look he had in the era that Matthew claimed to have represented him), a cut-down T-shirt revealing dark sleeves of ornate tattoos. He wore scuffed leather trousers and cowboy boots. He was dressed for the stage at Madison Square Garden, not a car park somewhere in the Valley. In half-light and shadow the effect was unsettling; it suddenly struck me that I didn't know where I was, or even who I was actually with, and I had a powerful urge to leave, to turn around and get in Iris's car and drive away from this. Instead I felt Donald's hand in the small of my back, guiding me forwards.

'What did I tell you?' he said. 'Fucking blows you away, doesn't it.'

Matthew stepped forwards too and offered his hand, which felt cold in mine. He held his head downwards, a diffident gesture that had none of the disdain and anger of the Nikki I'd met in London. That aside, could I have told them apart? Probably – Matthew was a few inches shorter and he lacked the palpable presence of the other Nikki, the strange set of rock-star genes that had given his skin and bones a powerful inner glow, and the sense that an outsider could only ever skitter across the surface of him. But that aside, yeah . . . yeah . . . one could have been the other, especially given the context of having the rest of the band around him.

Matthew said, 'H . . . h . . . hey . . .' His grip was weak and once I had let go of his hand he stepped backwards again, resting his arm on the open car door. He said nothing more.

'So,' said Donald. 'What do you think now? We're gonna win this lawsuit, right, kid?' He looked across at Matthew. 'And we're gonna get you what you deserve from those lying bastards. And then we're gonna make you a star. Because this kid writes real good songs. He wrote some that Mötley Crüe say they wrote, but they didn't, Matty wrote them. He's been fucked over real good, but now we're gonna fuck them right back.'

Matthew shuffled nervously and stared at the ground.

*

Later, trying to find my way out of the Valley in Iris's car, the faint and non-specific dread returned, a feeling that something bad was hiding just out of view. Donald had quickly realised that Matthew had no interest in going into the bar that we had just come out of dressed as he was (this was the Valley, not the Strip – most of the men in there looked like tough-guy Cholo steelworkers, a couple of whom had stared impassively at Donald's ponytail and ancient faded denims) and so we had sat inside Matthew's car, which Donald had got for him at the Rent-A-Wreck on Burbank, and Matthew had begun to talk, haltingly at first and constantly interrupted by Donald. While he did, his hands had gripped the steering wheel and he had looked at neither of us; instead he gazed through the windscreen across the empty car park. Matthew's story was a simple one at heart. He grew up in Erie, Pennsylvania, the adopted son of wealthy parents. He never felt that he belonged, to them or to the place. He'd gone off the rails as a teen, taking pot, flunking school, joining bands, stealing cars, and the first chance he got, he headed out to LA to become a rock 'n' roll star. It was much harder than he thought – it seemed as though every misfit from every small town in America had the same idea. He lived in his car, moving it from lot to lot in the hotels and supermarkets around West and North Hollywood, learning from the other kids which restrooms to wash and change in and how to talk the girls who hung out at the Roxy and the Rainbow into buying dinner or groceries. One evening he'd slipped into the Troubadour by tagging on to the end of a big party of record company freeloaders and he'd been sitting quietly at one of the tables at the back when he got talking to some old-looking guy who said that he was in a band who were kind of taking off. They had just signed a deal with Elektra. The guy seemed to have money, and it was no problem bumming drinks from him, and when he'd asked Matthew if he played guitar, Matt had said 'Sure.' They'd met on a couple more occasions, always at the Troubadour, where the guy, whose name was Mick, ensured Matthew could get in. One night, Mick was bummed out because his band had lost their bass player. He asked Matt if he could play bass, and Matt said 'Sure,' and the following evening he'd found himself in Doc McGhee's office playing four or five songs on some strange old instrument they'd given him. Afterwards he'd sat in reception for an age, and just as he was thinking he was probably supposed to head back down to the Troubadour or something and meet back up with Mick,

Doc had come back out and told him he was the new bass player in Mötley Crüe. Doc had put a bunch of papers down for him to sign, but when he'd started to write 'Matthew Trippe' Doc had stopped him and told him that his name was Nikki Sixx now, and that was the name he was to use. Matt didn't care. He already felt rich and famous; he'd write down whatever name they wanted, no problem. That's what he'd come to Hollywood for, right? He'd picked up the pen and signed, again and again, 'Nikki Sixx, Nikki Sixx, Nikki Sixx . . .'

And so, according to Trippe himself, the haunted double life of Matthew John Trippe had begun. There was lots more of course, lots more to come, but we hadn't begun with it yet, not in that car lot in the Valley. It was not the place and not the time, and I had no tape recorder and no pen, and anyhow I needed to get Matthew on his own, without Donald, who was already adding to the layers of manipulation and mediation in his story. Donald, with his big reveals and his big plans.

It was the small details that Matthew had given that stayed with me, that made the whole scene less preposterous. The way he said his arm had become infected after having copies of the other Nikki's tattoos inked over his existing ones (the tattooist had to dig so hard the deepest layers of skin and fat filled with pus and had to be drained). The pale but unmistakable scars from his facial surgery (said to be the removal of various 'imperfections' – again insisted upon and paid for, he said, by Doc). The wig he said he wore until his hair had grown the way that 'Nikki's' hair was supposed to look. The speech therapist that he had seen to try and eradicate his stammer (it had almost worked, but there was still a noticeable hitch when he was stressed by his memories).

As I thought about Matthew and what I was going to do

next I took the wrong ramp off the freeway and when I attempted to double back on myself lost any sense of direction and I was soon on dark and quiet streets, driving aimlessly around hoping to hit an intersection or find a sign but pretty soon it all began to look the same, long strips of industrial units: auto parts shops, motorcycle garages, warehouse supplies. The land was so flat and the night so dark that I couldn't see the hills and it wasn't until I forced away my unease and drove in a straight line in one direction that the geography began to change a little and I saw a sign to Calabasas, miles away from where I wanted to be but at least an escape route from the Valley. As the 101 finally began to climb into the canyons, I started to spook myself even more, imagining someone – a presence – there in the back seat of the car (someone or something that had got in and waited while I'd been with Donald and Matthew), half expecting to see its face each time I checked the rear-view mirror. Then more thoughts of Blair's brother in his ditched car, a dumped body left by killers; Blair alone in the mansion he would never return to, picturing her there as I glanced up at the lights of the houses that glowed far away from the steep roadsides. I touched the accelerator a little harder, anxious now to be back down on the Strip. Iris was waiting and I had a strong urge to be with her, to climb into the bed next to her and pull her close, wake her gently and tell her how crazy this place was and how glad I was to be back with her again. I turned up the radio and searched for something calming. A DJ was playing Christopher Cross, so I stuck with that through the tight hairpins down into Hollywood and on to Sunset, under the giant billboard that still said 'Disappear here'.

*

Marty had decided to hold a showcase for Lana, to announce her arrival in LA and to get her in front of A&R men, bookers, club owners, DJs and writers. He didn't want to put her on at one of the clubs on the Strip (part of his 'overarching strategy' to present her as 'somewhat above the norm'), so instead he'd decided to use his family's estate in Coldwater Canyon, a now-prime location above Beverly Hills that his father had acquired in the 1950s, adopting the location, he said, as a 'metaphor for where Lana's career would take her, high above the rest'. (Sylvio's response: 'He's fucked in the head – but it is a nice place, so we're not saying no . . .')

All of this came to me from Iris. On the trip to the desert, Marty had realised that she was both working for a record company and, like him, was a child of LA money, a part of his rare echelon, and since then he'd been calling her frequently – twice while I was out with Donald and Matthew – to run his ideas past her and to fuss over who he should invite.

'He's funny,' Iris told me. 'He makes me laugh,' but in what way she didn't say.

Marty had decided to have the show at dusk on a little stage he'd had erected on the canyon side below the house, one that offered a spectacular view out over the distant valley.

Iris had driven us out there in the early afternoon under another blameless sky. The summer didn't seem to want to end. She had on her crocheted hat and another short skirt. I watched those legs working the pedals. Iris smiled when she noticed. We came off the Coldwater Canyon road on the point of a tight bend and pulled on to a private driveway with some huge iron gates that swung open as we approached. Iris giggled. The hat threw freckled shadows on to her face.

'Ooh,' said Iris when she caught sight of the house, which

towered above us at the top of the drive, a vast one-level place shaped to the contours of the hill.

'Look at that, even the rich girl is impressed,' I said.

Iris parked in the shaded car bay. A maid led us through the house and out to the pool, which sat on a huge concrete deck that jutted out over the canyon edge. Marty procured Iris immediately and led her off by the hand to look at the stage and the arrangements. As she went, Iris turned around and raised her eyes and skittered off with tiny steps.

'My husband and your girlfriend, eh? We'll have to put a bloody stop to that.'

I looked around. Lana was on a lounger in the deep shade cut across the pool deck by the roof of the house. She reached behind herself to fasten her bikini top and walked over. 'Hey,' she said, her body cool as she hugged me. She smelled of sun oil and cigarettes. She felt ripe and heavy.

'Don't be bloody thinking that,' she said, reading my mind, and I laughed.

'We could get away with it, over there in the shade. We've got time.'

'You're not in my league, sunshine.'

She was right, but then I wasn't in Iris's league either. In truth, even had I been, whatever was needed to make it happen between Lana and me was missing, and we both knew it. That's why we could talk it up.

'Come with me, I need another ciggie before all this shit starts. I'll have a shower after. I don't want him smelling smoke on me.'

She led me to a little wooden deck concealed from the pool by the geography of the canyon's edge, where there was just about enough room for us to stand side by side. At first I couldn't see why it was there – it was too small to be any use in a place like this – but after Lana lit her cigarette and took a long drag, she extended her arm, using the glowing tip to point across the valley.

'This was Marty's father's favourite spot,' she said. 'The sun goes down right between those two hilltops over there. For about a minute the last bit of light comes right at you, even as it's dark on either side. It's beautiful. He used to come out here after he got back home from a hard day of fucking people over and watch it happen . . .' She laughed and took another drag on the cigarette.

'What was he like?'

'Tough . . . I dunno, I met him a couple of times, that's all. Marty and I were only just together when he died. He was old . . . His hands used to shake, I remember that. The ice rattling in his glass. He could hardly get it up to his mouth. It made me sad for him. Apparently the first thing he said to Marty after I'd left the room was, "Well, you finally got something right . . ." I think that's why he's stuck with me.'

She smoked for a little longer.

'It's why Marty's so angry and so fucking ambitious. Whatever he does, his dad would always have done it better. Everyone in this town knew his father, the lawyer. It's like he's still alive. So Marty decides he'll be a lawyer too, and work in the music business. I've said to him, we should just do something else . . . anything . . . open a restaurant. I dunno. Executive-produce films that never get made like every other fucker here does. I wouldn't care . . .'

She pulled greedily on the last of the cigarette butt. 'I do love him, you see . . .'

She looked softer now, more like the girl I remembered from England.

'But he's not listening. He's proving himself to the ghost of his father. I know it's good for me too, but it doesn't make him happy.'

The cigarette was finished. Lana lit another.

'You sure you want that . . .' I said, half joking.

'You've heard me sing enough times. A couple of ciggies aren't going to matter. I can't sing. David Lee Roth can't sing. Vince Neil can't sing . . .'

'That's true.'

'I'll shake my tits and do the usual. It's worked so far, hasn't it?'

I had to admit she was right.

'I've got Marty on one side of me and Sylvio on the other. He's just as bad. So I'll smoke if I want to. And I do want to.'

We looked out at the view while she did so. The band began to soundcheck, the noise echoing upwards from somewhere beneath us. Lana's bare foot tapped on the deck in time with the thump of the drums.

'Sylvio's as bad?'

'Course he fookin' is,' she said. 'Ever since we were little kids, this has been his fantasy. It's been happening in his head for years. Now he thinks that it's happening for real.'

'Do you think it is?'

'Not sure,' she said. 'Maybe.'

She smoked, slowly. We stood in silence while she did.

'I better go,' she said after a while. She dropped the cigarette butt, flattened it with her toe and flicked it between the wooden slats of the deck. She turned to leave but then stopped.

'I sound ungrateful, don't I?'

'Yes.'

Lana smirked. 'Maybe I am,' she said, and disappeared into the darkness of the house.

*

I wandered back to the pool deck. The water was an impossible, shimmering aqua that rippled slightly in the breeze. The noise from the soundcheck had stopped, and in the stillness the house felt almost abandoned. It was difficult to imagine living this way, high on the canyon top in the eerie silence, with all that life teeming down below. There were some beers chilling in an icebox by the poolside bar, so I took one and went inside the house, which was on a series of mini levels, each huge room separated from the next by two or three steps that gave the impression that you were floating from one to another. Each was expensively and tastefully furnished, all deep leather and polished wood, discreet art on the walls, abstract in one room, tribal in another, a family portrait in a third (Marty just a kid, his father's hand resting on his shoulder), and every now and again I came upon a long corridor that had rooms spinning off it: a games room, a den, a study, bathrooms and wetrooms and showers. The kitchen seemed to be hanging from the canyon edge, a dizzying view from the full-length windows, a series of islands adrift on the flagstone floor, each laden with stools and with cooking implements hanging above them from gleaming steel racks. Twenty people could have lived here quite comfortably and barely seen one another. Instead, as I understood it, the house was used periodically by Marty and his brother and sister while issues of a long-disputed probate ran endlessly on, and there was a small and silent staff living somewhere on the property and tending to it, but for the most part it stood silent and empty.

That desolation was almost palpable. I could feel it, deep in the shadows of these cool, dark rooms.

I picked one of the corridors hoping that it would lead outside and towards the stage, and instead I stumbled on a library with floor-to-ceiling shelves and polished ladders on runners to reach the highest of them. Like much of the rest of the house, the library seemed to have fallen from use a decade ago. There were runs of hardback fiction, first editions from what I could tell, of Updike, Bellow, Carver, Mailer, Styron, Faulkner and Irving. Hemingway was there, of course, and someone with humour had shelved Capote next to Vidal. I took some down. They didn't appear to have been moved from the shelves in years. They were tucked uniformly against one another, squeezed in. A couple of the Carvers were signed, and *Answered Prayers* was dedicated 'To Frank' in Capote's tiny hand. I pulled them out one by one and looked at them, held them, treasure after treasure – well at least to me. One shelf held a dozen Harold Robbins paperbacks. I pulled one of those out too. Its pages were waterstained and warped, read by the pool and left out in the sun to dry. It was the most life I could find in the place, along with the old leather chair set under a standing lamp which was cracked with wear but now, like everything else in sight, polished and deadeningly clean. I decided to reclaim it for whoever had built this library and loved this room – Marty's father most probably, a man who was rising ever higher in my estimation – and sat in the chair with the copy of *Rabbit, Run*. I read the section where Rabbit leaves his wife and drives all night to see his high-school basketball coach. The coach arranges a double date and Rabbit goes back with one of the women for a perfunctory and emotionless fuck in her rented room. It sent a little shiver through me. I imagined Marty's father screwing his way through every secretary, assistant and waitress he could lay his hands on and then coming home and sitting here remembering, going back over them in his mind, his wife, the tiny, red-headed woman at the front of their family portrait, alone elsewhere in the house. I pushed the book back on to the shelf, aligning its spine with all of the others.

*

A few hours later, a party raged through the house. It had an exultant force created by the post-gig euphoria – the showcase had gone about as well as it could have done, the air cool, the lights from the stage illuminating the trees and rocks that surrounded it in a series of colours, lending the quotidian nature of the music a skewed, almost haunted quality that it didn't really possess. Marty's plan was odd, but it had sort of worked. He'd sequestered the industry people on to a small seating platform with an elevated view of the stage, the handful of minor-league A&R scouts and club bookers and agents plus some faces from the Strip: Riki Rachtman, Bill Gazzarri, Stevie Rachelle, and a couple of free-press writers – 'opinion formers' as Marty had optimistically told Iris. He'd tried to get me to sit there too, but instead Iris and I had stood high at the back and looked down on the small crowd that Marty had bussed in from the Strip with the promise of free beer and a free show. The free beer had been waiting on the coach, so by the time Lana came on, it was a raucous gathering, perfectly primed for the unapologetic sexual frankness of her act. She had worn a low top and tiny shorts and performed her jiggling dance at the front of the stage, her voice breathy and insubstantial but well suited to the message she was trying to put across. The drunk kids had made a raucous noise while she did it. I had to hand it to Marty: against the odds, it was all vaguely convincing, as authentic as plenty of the bands I got paid to watch in the clubs of West Hollywood.

After the show was finished, people made their way up to the house, which, lit up, hung like a sculpture on the canyon top. I was amazed that Marty hadn't corralled the crowd back on to their bus, but he and Iris felt that if they came up to the house and had a good time and felt like insiders they would go back down to the Strip and sow the seeds, disseminate the vibes, make the buzz happen.

It sounded like a risk to me, but what did I know about human nature or anything else. Marty had the confidence of the rich. Iris and I sat in lounging chairs on the pool deck holding cold beers and watched it all happen. Music thundered through the open doors. Waitresses were dressed as sexy vampires and she-wolves. They carried silver cocktail trays that were being emptied as quickly as they could bring them out. A guy wearing leather chaps with nothing underneath, his bare ass in full view, stood right in front of us, talking loudly to a coterie of laughing girls.

'That's Randy,' Iris said. 'He's in that band Odin.'

'What band Odin?'

'You know Odin . . .'

'Do I? I think I'd remember Randy if I'd seen him. How come you know Odin?'

'They're that band.'

'Are you drunk?'

'Hmmmm,' she said. 'Yes, I am quite. Are you?'

Iris leaned forwards and poked Randy's ass several times with the end of her beer bottle, gently at first but then more and more firmly until he turned around, his face blank, as if this was a perfectly normal method of attracting his attention. Maybe it was.

'Hey Randy,' Iris almost yelled.

'Hey . . .' Randy gave Iris a shit-eating smile while he tried to remember who she was. '. . .'

'Iris,' said Iris.

'Iris, right . . . Hey. What's going on?'

'Having some beers.'

'Cool, man . . . party hardy yeah. Hey I know you. You're with that record company right?'

'You're real smart, Randy,' Iris yelled, and then started giggling to herself. She was drunker than I'd thought. Randy looked amiably dumb.

'Chugalug, baby,' he said, and took a long suck on his beer.

'Chugalug, Randy,' said Iris, and began laughing silently, tears forming in the corners of her eyes.

One of the girls he was with put her hand on his shoulder and glared at Iris. 'Hey don't talk to that bitch, Randy, she laughing at you.'

'She's okay,' Randy said. 'Her record company wants to sign us to a deal, right?'

This seemed to tip Iris over the edge.

'Yeah, Randy. We're gonna sign Odin right up. Million-dollar deal. Be in the office on Monday morning . . .'

Iris rose to her feet. She swayed. She clanked her beer bottle against Randy's.

'See you, Rand . . .'

I followed Iris inside. '(Don't Fear) The Reaper' swept through the house at high volume. Iris put her arms around my neck and began an unsteady dance. In my ear she said: 'I can still see Randy's ass . . .'

I span her around. She was right. Randy's ass was pressed up against the glass doors that separated the living area from the pool.

'Randy's ass gets everywhere,' I said.

'So I hear . . . That's how he gets all his gigs at Gazzarri's. Bill pretends he likes girls, but really he likes boys. He thinks Randy is the next David Lee Roth . . .'

Iris had gone from shouting to murmuring into my ear. I felt her weight against me. She stared drunkenly around the room. 'I have to tell you a secret . . .' she said, but when I asked her what it was, she just closed her eyes and placed her finger to her lips.

*

The night became fragmented, a series of scenes from a movie with no real plot. Instead it had a loosely connected cast of characters with the house itself at its centre. The darkness at the top of the canyon was almost total, the giant trees blotting most of the light from the distant Valley, the glow from the party quickly absorbed by the yawning black. The wind got up, rustling the palm leaves, blowing through the open doors and windows and adding to a slightly spooky vibe created by the sense of separation we had from the city. We were there but we were not.

Scene one began with a single tracking shot of Iris and me going from room to room, her with an arm around my shoulder, still giggling and unsteady – she was a mischievous but good-hearted drunk, alternating between knowing cheek and a sweet earnestness – her mind set on fun but her body ready to collapse. We found a large and uninhabited bedroom at the far end of one of the corridors, furnished in deep browns, with a vast round bed and door that locked from the inside (the story that Iris had told me that night in the Palisades weighed heavily on me) and she fell back on to the bed, sleep not far away. It was early yet, but Iris had been drinking all day. My plan was to go and find a book from the library and come back to this quiet sanctuary (the bedroom was so far-flung that the music and the noise from the party was audible only if you actually tried to hear it). I told her to lock the door behind me and listen for my knock.

'I will,' she said, and as I left I heard the key turn in the lock behind me.

The camera followed as I looked for the library, but it wasn't where I remembered it being, and soon I was handed another beer by a sexy vampire waitress and from behind her someone shouted my name and when I turned around I saw Sylvio and Tony standing with a couple of girls, one of whom was waving a bottle of champagne and dancing suggestively.

'These two chicks are krelled out of their minds,' Sylvio said. 'They both want to suck our cocks, don't you girls?'

The girls nodded.

'That's why we're in this business, innit. We're going to find a room in a minute.'

'We are if you get us another bump,' said one of the girls. 'No bump, no hump.'

'No blow, no go . . .' the other giggled.

'Their pussies get wet for champagne and cocaine . . .' said Sylvio. They all laughed at this. They looked crazed and ghosted, too far gone to do anything other than talk, so I left them and carried on the search for the library.

Then in a series of short, soft-focus scenes with their blurred edges and underwater dialogue, as the camera moved through the chattering, wired groups of kids talking too loudly and posing too hard, oddly adrift in this luxury, I came upon Marty, deep in conversation with a couple of guys I vaguely recog-nised, promoters maybe, bookers who could offer buy-ons for mid-range tour support. All of a sudden he looked like what he was, smart, monied, saturnine, in control of his natural environment, far more so than he ever did when he was running around after the band or driving us out to the desert. He raised his glass and offered an implacable smile as he saw me pass by.

Next came Randy, still loud but slurring now, and, just as Iris had predicted, with Bill Gazzarri standing close to him and sneaking lascivious glimpses of his ass. 'He's gonna be a star,' Bill was saying, his voice rasping, his face partly hidden by the white fedora hat he always wore. 'You mark my words. That Randy, he's a foxy guy . . .'

The camera wobbled through more rooms, the music quieter in their vast spaces, and in shaded corners it picked up dope being passed and shared, a few couples getting it on. At one of the island worktops in the kitchen, a group of sexy vampire and she-wolf waitresses were sat smoking cigarettes, their work done.

'Hello,' one of them said. 'Can I get you something?' She stood up and slid one foot back into her high shoe.

'No, no . . . I've had enough . . .' I waggled the empty bottle of beer I was holding and set it down on the counter top. 'I'm just, you know, wandering around . . .'

'Amazing place, isn't it?' she said. 'We do a lot of this shit, but I've never been this high up the canyon before. So, how come you're here?'

I gave her a quick precis of how I knew Marty and Lana and Sylvio.

'Cool,' she said. 'That must be interesting . . . kind of . . . Do you write movies?'

'No, nothing like that. Are you an actress then?'

'When I get the chance, sure.' She smiled and came a little

closer. 'For a hundred, you can have a private audition tonight, hon.'

She was a beautiful girl. She smelled of perfume and cigarette smoke and beer. Her lipstick was smudged in the corners of her mouth, the honeyed skin of her breasts disappearing into the white folds of her blouse. For a moment I felt the pull of her, the sharp desire for an alien body.

'Hey, I'd love to but I don't have a hundred and my girlfriend is asleep in one of the bedrooms . . .'

'Cool, another time then, hon,' she said. 'Take this . . .' She slid a card into my hand and slipped back to her friends in a slow dissolve, me realising, as I left the kitchen and floated down the hallway to a high vaulted room empty save for a couple of people passed out on couches, that I'd begun thinking of Iris as my girlfriend. I slipped the card into the pocket of my jeans and soon found myself back outside at the pool, where some girls had stripped to their underwear and were jumping into the water to the cheers of the guys who were egging them on, clapping and jeering. A couple were fucking quite openly by the steps in the shallow end, her ankles on his shoulders, each looking directly at the other, screwing in silence, their bodies invisible in the blue light of the water. It was like a scene from a spring break porno shot by David Lynch, the skewed atmosphere created by the cinematic setting, the heavy symbolism of its location, the strange mix of people in attendance and the way they were behaving, something that shouldn't have been possible but somehow was.

The final images were more fractured still, set in the darkened arterial corridors that threaded through the house. I was becoming increasingly tired and disorientated by then, a hangover already beginning to kick in even though I still felt quite drunk, a double-whammy I could have done without. I wandered down two passageways, convinced each time that this was the one on which I had found the room for Iris but neither were. I found another, this one less familiar than the other two. As I came to the rooms towards its end, I began twisting each handle to see if the door was locked. The final handle gave slightly but then resisted my push. I knocked on the door, gently at first but when there was no answer, more loudly. I heard some sort of movement from inside, a woman's voice, so I knocked again, more urgently this time knowing that Iris would almost certainly have been asleep by now and she might take some waking. The door opened a little and Lana's face appeared behind it, her hair dishevelled, her make-up smeared.

'Fookin' hell, love, what do you want?' she said.

'Sorry, wrong room. I, uh, I left Iris along here some-where . . . thought it was here.'

'Don't worry.' She hurriedly pulled the strap of her halter top up over her shoulder as she moved her hand to the side of the door. Through the darkness I heard a voice behind her, indistinct and low. 'Nothing, it's not . . .' she said, and as she did the door snapped firmly shut.

*

I woke on a stiff leather couch, my neck uncomfortably cramped where I'd fallen asleep against the hard padding of the armrest. Light was streaming through the window, hot and bright on my cheek, neon sundots burnt on to my retinas. I sat up slowly and looked around. I was in some sort of small and otherwise empty sitting room. I straightened up my clothes and wandered out, slightly surprised to discover that the room led into the library. I found my way out on to the pool deck, which was already warming up, the sun above the trees. I walked over to the rail and looked out over the Valley, laid out in its shimmering grids far below the canyon. Tiny cars moved soundlessly on the distant roads. The breeze felt sweet.

'Sleep okay?'

I turned around to see Marty walk out on to the deck behind me.

'Not really,' I said, rubbing at my neck. 'Crashed out on a couch somewhere I'm afraid. Where did everyone go?'

'We got them all back on the buses just after 1 a.m. Took a bit of wrangling. We had to fish a couple out of the pool. Found one guy wandering around the canyon down there' – he pointed airily to some of the scrubland beneath the deck – 'had to pour cold water over a few, but that was okay. No damage done . . .'

The cleaners had been busy too. The deck was spotless.

'What about you, Marty?'

He grinned. 'I haven't been to bed yet. I . . .' He stopped for a moment, obviously thinking better of what he was about to say. We stood in silence for a while.

'I found the library yesterday,' I said. 'It's amazing . . .'

'My father's,' he said. 'All his books. When I was a kid he used to let me sit in there with him while he read. Had a little chair made for me just like his . . . My brother's a writer, you know.'

'Is he? What kind?'

'Books, screenplays. All unpublished or unmade, as far as I know. We don't speak often. We, uh, we disagree about what to do with this place for a start.'

'What did your father think, about him being a writer?'

Marty gave a brittle laugh.

'My father . . . my father, let's say, wasn't entirely convinced by the direction either of us took. We have a sister too. She was the one he thought had got it right.'

'What does she do?'

'She invests his money. Or at least she did. Now she invests her money . . .'

Marty let the conversation hang. After a few moments the housemaid came out and laid a table for breakfast, placing a steaming coffee pot down on a starched tablecloth. I wondered if Marty had always lived this way. It seemed as though he had. He invited me to sit with him. The coffee was hot and bitter on the tongue. Soon Iris came out and joined us. She looked gloriously pale under her hat. She kissed Marty on the cheek and then me gently on the lips. Her skirt slid up a little as she sat, and she fussed with it for a moment.

'So how are you boys?' she asked.

*

The maid brought us sliced fruits and fresh pastries, warm pancakes with syrup and bacon, poached eggs with hollandaise sauce, scrambled eggs with Tabasco sauce, creamed grits, French toast, several cereals, a jug of yoghurt, milk, honey . . . It kept coming.

'Last night was awesome,' said Iris. I thought she might be joking but she was impassive, neutral. She and Marty looked at one another and laughed. She placed some fruit on her plate.

'I think we're going to get some offers,' said Marty.

'For sure. I mean, did you see . . .'

They talked on. I began to zone out. I was tired and

hungover. Fragments of the night ran through my head as I stared out over the canyon. The sexy vampire waitress. The momentary want. Iris asleep in her locked room. The endless corridors. Lana coming to her bedroom door, her top slipping down. A dark shadow, quickly covered. Another sharp stab of want. The first time I'd felt that with Lana, so different from England. England, where she was a joke, a vacuous mag pin-up getting by on her looks. Here, where she was something else.

'You're not in my league, sunshine.'

The voice behind her in the room.

Marty: 'I haven't been to bed yet.'

Fragments and snatches. Marty and Iris. Marty and Lana. Lana and Doug. Sylvio and Tony. Iris and Randy.

I closed my eyes. The wind blew. More fragments. The couple fucking in the blue water. Randy's ass.

'Randy, they're calling you stupid.' Randy: 'Hey, that's okay.'

A kid came out to clean the pool. He had a net and a bag of chemicals. He took off his flip-flops and scooped the net through the water. Down below, a couple of gardeners were combing through the scrub, throwing trash into black bags. Marty and Iris seemed oblivious to them. Iris laughed at something Marty said.

'He's funny . . . he makes me laugh . . .'

Sylvio on Marty: 'He's fucked in the head.'

Lana on Sylvio: 'He's just as bad . . .'

Fragments and moments. I knew that alcohol contracted the brain, shut sections of it down, but sometimes it opened a pathway and allowed the mind to just *reach*: the smell of the sexy vampire waitress – perfume and cigarette smoke and spilled beer.

'Do you write movies?'

The sweetness of Iris, drunk.

'I have to tell you a secret . . .'

Iris in the ghost town. Blair in the Palisades. Blair's brother in the hills.

'This is LA . . . no one dies without a rumour.'

Donald and Matthew. Matthew and Nikki. Nikki and Doc. Doc and me.

'You are one sick puppy, buddy.'

★

The pool boy pulled something out of the filter. 'Hey boss,' he said, and held up some women's underwear. 'Here's the problem.'

Marty nodded. 'You better clean the whole thing.'

'Someone had a good time, then,' said Iris.

Marty stared at the water. Something came to me.

'You don't need a record company, Marty. The only reason to sign to a big label now is to make yourself feel good. They'll give you, what, $200,000 to make a record? Recoupable, of course, and you won't recoup unless they put a marketing budget behind it, which they won't. It'll just be a punt with their spare change – money that they would otherwise pay in tax. You'll get offered some second-rank tour support slot with a massive buy-on, which they'll advance you, also recoupable. They'll rent the tour bus and the gear and pick up the hotels and charge them all back to you. If they take up the option on a second album, they'll give you another advance, probably a quarter of what they gave you the first time, and add that to the debt. You'll have to write it really quickly because you've been on the road for nine months playing to half-empty arenas that can't wait for you to get off so the good band can come on. If the second record doesn't fly, you won't be able to get hold of anyone on the phone, and you'll get a lawyer's letter couriered over telling you that you've been dropped. You won't get another deal because no one wants damaged goods and there are 6,000 other bands on the Strip to choose from that look just like you did before you got fucked over and became second-hand.'

Marty looked up at me. 'So what, then . . . ?'

'You've got money, right? Anyone can see that. Pay a few thousand dollars to a studio around here. Make a record in two weeks. Do it fast, rough and ready. Get it pressed up and put it out yourself. Go to a distributor and get it in every record shop in LA. Hire a radio plugger for a week and get some plays. Hand out flyers on the Strip. Pack out Gazzarri's for a couple of nights and get a buzz going . . .'

No one said anything, so I went on.

'Mötley Crüe did that. *Too Fast For Love*, on Leathür Records, Doc got them signed to Elektra. Great White did it, Alan Niven got them on EMI. Guns N' Roses – *Live Like a Suicide*, signed to Geffen within a week. Then you've got a chance.'

The pool boy was throwing some sort of powder into the water. The tang of ammonia. He attached a small motor to the filter and the water began to churn through the blades, making little whitecaps on the surface. Gulls flew low over it. Their sharp, sad cries. No record ever made that could catch a feeling like that.

'*David Lee Roth can't sing. Vince Neil can't sing.*'

'You and Doc are quite similar, Marty.'

'Are we?'

'In one way, yes. Doc didn't get into the music business to get rich. He already had money. People can sense when you're not desperate. They know that you mean it when you tell them to fuck off. Let Sylvio and Tony and Doug be desperate. Let Lana be desperate. The bands have to be. You don't.'

★

More unreadable silence. Marty poured coffee. Ah well, fuck him. You could lead a horse to water and all that. And this was LA. What did I know? I'd fluked my way here like everyone else. Only people like Marty belonged, would grow old here. Being old in LA – how was that? Because you never saw them did you, the old in LA. Where were they? What happened to them? Where did they go, LA's old? Where did they disappear to, when they could no longer look like everyone else?

Sylvio came out, blinking in the light, sliding his sunglasses down from the top of his head. He sat down, poured coffee, put his head in his hands.

'Fookin' hell. It's a young man's game, innit.'

He was given to statements like this one. They made perfect sense to him, chiming with the dialogue in his head. He looked up.

'The problem with this place is that it's too good . . .' I said. 'The problem with this place is that it's impossible to begin a sentence with the words "the problem with this place" . . .'

Once, I'd spent a day with Sylvio in his home town, far in the north of England, a port town, a set of docks on a bleak estuary, the suspension bridge over the river bending under a weak sun. We drove into the heart of the port so that he could show me the narrow streets, battered and defeated, the puddles from the rain apparently immune to light, the cranes on the docks towering above the houses. We passed a long-closed cinema, its facade eroded by years of rain and wind straight in from the sea. It was where it had begun for Sylvio. He'd watched the film of Woodstock there, he saw Hendrix and Santana and he knew what he was going to do, what he was meant to become.

I pulled the car over and we got out. The doors of the cinema were chained together, the windows boarded up. There was a convenience store on the corner, and a desperate pub. Everyone in it seemed to be either sixteen or fifty. There was no in between. In places like this you were young and then you were old.

Where do they go, the old?

We crossed the suspension bridge on the way out, Sylvio not looking back. No one looked back at places like that. His family had got out. His mother over the river, Lana and Sylvio to London and then to here. There was no thought of returning. The only thing worse than not escaping a town like that was having to return to it.

The problem with this place . . .

Doc and Marty. Matthew and Sylvio. This place. This city.

★

That day remains in my mind even now, Lana and Tony and Doug coming out to join us, stories being told, breakfast becoming lunch (the same maid, more trays and plates and bowls, heaped and loaded), the great orb of the sun illuminating the canyon and the valley beyond – from up here, the earth actually glowed – it was utterly magnificent. It was impossible not to feel melancholy about it, then or now, because it was one of those days that was perfect in its way. I suppose that was the difference between people like Marty and me: they expected their lives to continue like this indefinitely, just the faces around them changing. I knew that for me, it would pass. That was why Sylvio raged to hold on to it. He reminded me of a shark, always moving forwards, always moving away from where it had come (the shark's life – an endless forward journey . . .). Forwards and west to here. There was almost nowhere further.

Where do they go, the old? Where do they go?

Iris drove us back to the house just off Fountain, having decided that her self-imposed exile was over after a couple of nights at the Hyatt. She was lighter again, back to herself. The place felt empty as we walked through the door, and it was: Brenna nowhere to be found, and the housemates now moved out. It was dusk. We sat on a lounger on the deck by the giant palm, Iris curled up against me.

'So what happened to you last night? I was horny . . .'

'You were sleepy.'

'Sleepy and horny.'

'I'm sorry. It was the size of that house. I ended up on a couch somewhere.'

'Well, you missed out.'

'I know . . .'

She began pulling off her clothes, tumbling out of them towards me, her skirt riding up, her pale, soft body in my arms in the dark garden, the sight and smell of her all-consuming, and yet when I closed my eyes – *how, why?* – I saw Lana at the door, hitching her top, the sexy vampire waitress smoking cigarettes, some girl being fucked in a swimming pool . . . Brenna at her party, changing . . .

Ah Iris, I'm sorry. Welcome to this foul junkyard of my heart . . .

After, Iris put on her vest and lay by my side, her eyes dark surrounded by dark.

'So you did like that?' she said. 'Do you like anyone else?'

'What?'

'Is there anyone else? Because Marty told me that he saw you with a girl last night.'

'Did he . . . Who does he think I am, Vince Neil?'

She giggled. 'It was a waitress.'

'What was he doing, following me? That guy is weird.'

'So were you?'

'No I wasn't. And even if I had been, she wanted to charge me for it . . .'

Iris punched my arm.

'What do you mean?'

'She asked me if I had a hundred bucks . . .'

She was laughing now, despite herself.

'That never happens to Vince Neil,' I said.

'I guess it doesn't.'

'You have to ask yourself what your pal Marty was doing hiring hookers for his party.'

She said nothing. I stroked the top of her head.

'Let's go inside,' she said. 'It's getting cold.'

6. The Marina

A few days later we were in a little recording studio in Marina del Rey, a lo-rise breezeblock cave, windowless and anonymous, a few streets from the water. Marty had booked it. There had been no hint that it was anything other than his idea, all part of a plan long in the making, but I was hardly bothered by that. What with the Chloride City trip and the showcase in the canyon and now Lana making a record, it had become a strong enough story for the magazine to cover in some depth (I could feel it too – maybe through Lana I could somehow suggest some wider and more universal themes, about LA and its thousands of outsiders, all reaching for a higher reality that they could see every day and yet that stayed miles out of reach. Geoff just thought it was funny that she was making a record in two weeks), and this, along with the looming madness of Matthew Trippe and a couple of small pieces that kept the hotel room ticking over, meant that I'd cancelled my return flight (it was about to expire anyway) and hadn't yet bought another. It also meant that Marty was giving me a per diem, a joyous start to each morning.

Marty had struck a deal with the studio owner for fourteen days of its downtime, essentially daylight hours (there was a prevailing myth that recording should be done at night, an idea that had arisen, as far as anyone could tell, for the reason that bands with the budget to book studios out for months on end spent the mornings in bed and the afternoons getting drunk and stoned before the fabled 'creative urge' descended with nightfall, at which point they began, through the long, chemical hours, to finally get something down on to tape). Marty was temperamentally unsuited to that argument, and Tony, who was nominally 'producing' (the desk was being driven by a hyperactive, wired little tape-op called Fast Eddie), and Sylvio were just happy to be making a record in LA in 1988, and so Marty had the studio until six each night, at which point it was taken over by a grim speed metal band from San Francisco who were demoing for Capitol records and who, Fast Eddie said, were strung out on the cheap heroin that was flooding through the downtown areas of the city, and were alternately surly and aggressive or nodding out (Fast Eddie reckoned he was doing most of the guitar overdubs himself while they were semi-conscious in the playback lounge).

Sylvio had taken up a position behind the desk, sitting on the left, with Eddie in the middle and Tony on the right. They remained there pretty much all day every day, drinking coffee from the place over the road, Sylvio subtly engineering a sound that brought the guitars higher and higher in the mix (or so he thought: Eddie told me during one of his rare ventures beyond the control room – missions that usually involved him throwing down fast food and making calls on the studio payphone to a sad-eyed girl from Lomita – that he waited for the speed metal band to nod out each night and then readjusted Sylvio's mixes).

Sylvio hadn't noticed, and nor had anyone else. It was impossible to, in the general racket that Eddie was wrangling down on to tape and bouncing from channel to channel, because, as with most studios, everything was played back at an intense and terrifying volume that smothered everything else. It was partly why all records sounded good in the studio – they were too loud to sound bad.

I'd seen some bands take six months to get a drum sound. Def Leppard, for example, had needed five *years* to make *Hysteria*, not that they cared as it now shimmered unavoidably from every radio station in America, a study in immaculate sterility, but that luxury was unavailable to Lana. Eddie had simply set them up on the first morning and had them play through each song as live several times, patching together a master of each and then adding overdubs and backing tracks before having Lana in to record vocal tracks and Sylvio the guitar solos (Tony had been allocated one, a short outro piece that he would play with some fire, Sylvio keen to bring the faders down on it as soon as possible for reasons of 'running time'). It wasn't the way it would be done with time and money, but it was a pretty fail-safe method, and it meant that any raw energy that was present would be caught on the tapes.

It also allowed Sylvio and Tony to prevaricate endlessly as they lived out their studio fantasies, Fast Eddie wearily trying to edge them towards consensus over a rim-shot or a bass run or middle eight, his pin-bright pupils and busy hands moving rapidly in the studio gloom.

He had each of the song titles written on masking tape and stuck to the desk above the various faders and knobs that controlled them. Here was Lana's world view, her artistic statement: 'Gypsy Dancer'; Rock 'n' Roll Lady'; 'All Falling Down'; 'Jealous Heart'; 'Broken Down Angel'; 'Public Enemy No. 1'; 'Gypsies and Rainbows'; 'Saturday Nite' ('That's a lot of gypsies,' Eddie had said, when he first saw the tracklisting, in an attempt to break the ice. Lana had simply stared at him until he looked away). The final song was called 'Sylvio's Surprise', an instrumental piece in the style of Santana, with congas, and jazzy bass parts played by Tony. Sylvio had no shame or self-consciousness about taking his cues from Santana's career. When Carlos had released an album called *Blues For Salvador*, Sylvio's next composition was called 'Cuba Libra'. Carlos had 'Angel of Sunlight', Sylvio had 'Angels of Earth'. 'Sylvio's Surprise', in turn, was sort of budget 'Samba Pa Ti', horribly out of place but apparently some sort of tacitly agreed pay-off between him and Lana.

Iris would drop me in the Marina each morning on her way to work and meet me in the evening, when we'd walk through the harbour to a little restaurant she knew and sit out by the boats as they tied up for the night. It was therapeutic to stay there in the cool air and enjoy the normality, the deadening ringing in my ears slowly subsiding, Iris telling stories of the many phone calls she was receiving each day from Marty, mimicking his voice with deadly accuracy as he asked about pressing plants and distributors and printers. During one call he'd wanted to know how to get one of the front-facing racks as you walked into Tower on Sunset (the answer was sell half a million records); in another how to get prime-time airplay on KNAC (pretty much the same – in fact it was the answer to almost every question he asked). Marty didn't really get how things worked at the bottom, it wasn't his life or his way. The aim for Lana's record, the best he could hope for, was simply to create the same kind of low-level buzz the kids on the Strip got through handing out flyers and playing endless first-on-the-bill slots at the Roxy and the Cathouse but instead to do it by having a record to give to club DJs and local-radio guys, to LA promoters and small record shops. There were hundreds of bands out there. A cool record on an indie label was a chance to elbow your way to the front and press your face up against the glass.

'We're going to take him to the Tropicana,' Iris said.

'We are?'

'Yes. Tomorrow night.'

Iris's eyes glittered. I laughed at her delight. The Tropicana was barely more than a strip joint. Every night they filled a big plastic pool with mud and had the girls wrestle each other. Lots of bands hung out there, and Vince Neil had got married to one of the wrestlers, a blonde hard-body called Sharise. Mötley Crüe had their records played all the time too. Getting a Tropicana dancer to strip to one of your songs was almost as good as getting airplay at local radio.

'He's not going to wear the suit, is he?'

'He kind of looks weird in jeans. I like his suits. He needs to be who he is. Anyhow, Brenna is coming too. She knows lots of the girls. She does all of their waxing and . . . stuff.'

'Stuff?'

'Girls' stuff. She bleaches their assholes too.'

'How do you bleach someone's asshole . . . ?'

'Jesus, with bleach. How do you think? It just looks nicer.'

'Nicer than what?'

'Nicer than sticking a dirty, hairy asshole in someone's face.'

'Well, when you put it like that . . . What a job she's got.'

'She's very good at it . . .'

'Wait, you don't . . . ?'

Iris smirked. 'What do you think? It looks good, doesn't it?'

'Okay, I'm a born-again fan of ass-bleaching. I want to see all of the bleached asses I can tomorrow. It'll be an education.'

Women and their intimacies – so distant, so apart. I wondered at them as I watched the last of the sail-boats tying up for the night.

★

The Tropicana was on North Western Avenue near the 101, its neon sign the only feature that distinguished it from the hundreds of other grey one-storey buildings that lined the avenues and boulevards of Los Angeles. Marty drove us there, wearing his suit.

'You're not going to be taking notes are you, Marty?'

'Fuck off.'

'Only it's hard to write when you've got a chick's bleached ass in your face . . .'

'Again, fuck off . . .'

'You're going to see a lot of those tonight. Bleached asses.'

Iris was in the back seat with Brenna, both drinking cans of beer.

'You seem to know a lot about it,' Brenna said.

'Oh yeah, Iris told me. I'm going to be admiring your artistry later.'

Brenna snorted. 'The Englishman is learning all about American asses,' she said. 'We know how to treat them right.'

Marty tugged the car sideways off the road and into the Tropicana parking lot. He got out without a word and marched towards the doors.

'Wow, he needs to relax a little,' said Brenna. 'Get that stick out from up his butt . . .'

Iris linked her arm through Brenna's and they followed Marty into the club. We walked upstairs, Brenna waving hello to several people, Iris stopping to kiss Dennis the MC, who immediately sent a big order of drinks over to the table we had, which was a couple of rows back from the mud-wrestling pit.

There were a surprising number of women sitting at the tables, watching the girls. Even stripping was going unisex. The girls were tall and big-breasted. They wore only G-strings and heels. Iris and Brenna and I sat and looked at them. The music was too loud for us to say much. Iris was pointing at the ones who had had tit jobs. Most of them had. That was fine by me. Their self-esteem seemed to be high.

Iris could be dispassionate about their beauty. As each one came to the tables near us, she leaned over and spoke into my ear.

'Great legs.'

'She's gorgeous.'

'She can dance.'

'Nice shoes.'

'Big ass.'

And so on. A couple of the girls smiled at Brenna. When Dennis got up to announce that the first bout of the evening was to begin, the crowd around the bar dispersed and people piled into the seats behind ours. I saw Taime and Brent from Faster Pussycat, who were surrounded by girls, and Tracii Guns was with Steven Adler talking to a couple of the dancers (ever since Sharise, who had been one of the most popular wrestlers, married Vince and then Vince had immortalised their love in a song called 'Girls Girls Girls' – 'Tropicana's where I lost my heart' ran the lyric – the place had a new cachet as a venue for rock star–dancer hook-ups). The girls walked to the front and lined up. The bouts were arranged via an audience auction. Dennis whipped up the bidding by giving each of the girls a wrestling name. The first bout was between 'Cactus Kelly' and the 'Red Snapper'. A group of guys had bought Cactus Kelly for $300. She stepped forward, and stepped out of her heels, bending down to run her hands along her legs, her hamstrings pulling tight as the muscles in her ass swelled and the little bikini string disappeared between them. She wiggled her backside to great cheers and then jumped into the mudpit. The Red Snapper was bought for

$300 too. She walked over to the group who'd won her auction and stood in front of them with her hands on her hips. Slowly she leaned forwards and beckoned for the cash, making as though to kiss one of the guys and then pulling back to more cheers. She jumped into the mudpit. The DJ cranked the music – 'Bathroom Wall' ('We got fuckin' Taime and Brent in the house tonight, fuckers . . .' he yelled) – and the girls ran at one another. They dived and span in the mud, which flew up all over the ceiling and over the people in the first rows, their bodies soon slick with it. They fought with abandon, pressing up hard against one another, the music virtually warping the walls with its volume, but the shouts and screams of the crowd still somehow audible above it.

The matches went on for an hour or so. The girls who weren't in the pit walked through the crowd selling kisses. If they got enough money, they would rub their breasts in a guy's face, or bend over in front of him and shake their ass. Marty watched it all impassively, the odd fleck of mud on his suit. Every time a big record came on, the crowd would get excited, and the girls would make more money.

Iris stood up and took my hand. Brenna led us through the club and up the stairs to a room where the dancers changed. The music caused the floor to thud under our feet. The girls walked around naked and unembarrassed. A couple sat on stools, staring vacantly into the room. They appeared exhausted, their mental and sexual energy spent. One of the DJs came in and Iris introduced him to Marty, who went into a long description of Lana and her record, and how much it would mean to her to hear it in the Tropicana (as far as I knew, she'd never set foot in the place). The DJ listened to about half of it and then said, 'Sounds cool, dude, whatever, just bring it on in when it's done, man.'

Marty smiled.

I thought of him on the deck of the house in the canyon. Some people could cross these divides. I wasn't sure that Marty was one of them. A dancer walked up to Brenna.

'Hey look at this,' she said, and pulled her panties to one side. 'What a mess, huh?'

Marty studied us for a moment. 'Let's go,' he said coldly.

★

'Did you like that?' Iris asked.

We were back at her place. Marty had driven us quickly down Santa Monica, the air con up, the radio on, Iris in the front seat next to him, their conversation inaudible beneath the 1970s soft rock which was in turn deadened by the deep leather seats and the thick glass of Marty's car, which was some kind of high-end limo with enough torque to press your head back into the cushion of the rest when he pushed his foot down to beat the lights. Brenna and I sat in the back, each staring out of a different window, distracted by the ever-changing mini movies of the streets.

Iris directed Marty on to Fountain. He left us there with barely a goodbye before heading back to the house in the canyon and Lana (they had surrendered the apartment in the Marina to Sylvio, Tony and Doug while they made the record – Lana had barely visited the studio since laying down the live tracks; she would come back in for the last couple of days to record the vocals, and she seemed deeply indifferent to the rest of the process).

We were sitting in the darkened, high-ceilinged lounge, the shadows from the giant palm making patterns on the walls, the only sounds the breeze that whistled through the great cracked leaves of the tree and the chirp of cicadas, and every time they died away, I could feel and hear the high ringing in my ears from the volume of the music in the club. Iris was curled in her favourite chair, while Brenna lay down on the couch, staring up at the ceiling and sipping on one of the iced glasses of vodka and lemonade that Iris had poured out.

'It was great,' I said. 'It was good to see some hot women at last.'

'Don't be smart . . . although they were quite hot, I agree.'

'Who did you like?' Brenna said.

'The Red Snapper.'

'Ooh, she's a bad girl. You wouldn't last long with her.'

'I don't think I'd last long with any of them. But I wasn't as scared as Marty.'

'He was terrified, wasn't he? Terrified that he might get a hard-on.'

'Aw, don't be harsh,' said Iris. 'It's just not his thing, poor Marty.'

'Yes, poor, tragic Marty. His life is so difficult. I'm always surprised when he makes it through a day. I bet his dad would have liked the Tropicana more than he did.'

I told Brenna about Marty's father, about the house and the library I'd found, the conversation drifting along as Brenna spoke about her own father, a domineering bully whom she no longer saw, and then tenderly about Iris's, her voice quiet and distant in the now-full darkness of the room, Iris curled up with her drink, not saying anything, her eyes closing, then mine too, just listening to Brenna in the dark until she had nothing more to say. I must have slipped into a lucid, fragmented dream in which we were back at the Tropicana and trying to find our way through a maze of empty rooms and to the exit, the music from the club thudding dully through the walls but never coming any closer.

I woke with a start. Iris was no longer in her chair. Brenna was on the couch. She lay on her side, one knee drawn to her chest. She appeared to be asleep, but as I got up, she opened her eyes.

'Ah shit,' she said. 'We should go to bed. Give me a hand . . .'

I pulled her up from the sofa. She put her arms around my neck and kissed my cheek. For a moment I felt the weight of her against me. It lasted a moment longer than it should have. She kissed my other cheek.

'Hey, you're not in the Tropicana now,' she whispered. 'Goodnight.'

'Goodnight Brenna,' I said, and watched her sway from the room.

★

Marty wanted me to go up to the house to interview Lana before she cut her vocal tracks. Sylvio decided to come too. He talked Marty into lending me his car. We went early one afternoon. Sylvio settled himself in the passenger seat, his window down, his shades on, fiddling with the radio. He listened for a while and then twisted the dial down. It was one of the things I liked about him. Most musicians, especially rock musicians, were desperate to impress with their taste, the 'influences' that had 'shaped' their sensibility. Given half a chance (on the tour bus, in the hotel room, in the limousine en route to the party) they would dig out their obscure blues, their ragtime jazz, their baroque chamber music and listen to it hard and in silence while I watched them do it. Bozo hair metallers who'd somehow hit the jackpot would talk to me about Nick Drake, Tim Buckley, John Coltrane, Leonard Cohen. Guys who'd spent desperate years living with ten other people in a two-bedroom dive in North Hollywood would claim that they'd been listening *to Pet Sounds* or *Exile on Main Street* or *Never Mind the Bollocks* or *Berlin*, which was strange because the only records I'd ever heard in places like that were *Van Halen I* and *Back in Black* and *Theatre of Pain*.

Sylvio sensed the ridiculousness of it all. The fantasy he had created for himself was a different one, and he wore his only influence openly. He had spent ten years being dismissed, lightly regarded, taken as a joke, but in turn he could see the joke that was all around him. We had some of our best times laughing about it, me or Ray telling him stories about interviews and photoshoots that had become ludicrous exercises in vanity and delusion (the self-obsessed singer of a Welsh glam band who spent two weeks in New York and came back with an American accent; the guitarists writing their symphonies; the drummers planning their concept albums). It was a madness that was everywhere.

If Sylvio had an image of himself, it was one that he lived, or at least that he tried to. The character he inhabited was an exaggeration of what was already there. We talked all the way up to the top of the canyon. I'd always been able to speak to Sylvio. Sometimes I pretended to ask myself why, but I knew it was because I could tell him anything and he would take it in his usual way, with a joke, a laugh; whatever I wanted to do, he'd usually say, 'Do it, I would,' and it was true, he would. He took simple decisions and accepted their consequences into his life. I told him about Iris, about Brenna, everything: the trip to see Iris's father, the Palisades, the party at Marty's, how Brenna had felt in my arms after the night at the Tropicana (a memory that provoked an uncomfortably sharp longing).

We talked about the girls who wrestled there and the sexy vampire waitresses (Sylvio and Tony had shared the rest of their blow with a couple of them and had a carnal, druggy night in one of the vast bedrooms).

'It's just sex, man', Sylvio said. 'The more you fuck, the more you want to fuck. We're in LA. Everyone's doing it . . .'

'Well, maybe. Except for Marty.'

'He's a weird cat, that's true.'

'Is he still worried about Doug and Lana?'

'Marty's worried about everything. It's always going to be that way. Lana's a beautiful girl, and he's not a fookin' great-looking guy. It's the way of the world. Rich guys get them, and then they have to worry about them. Silly bastard,' he said. 'I love him though.'

'I bet you do.'

Sylvio gave me a look of fake shock. 'What are you trying to say . . . ?' He smiled and gave another of his gnomic statements: 'It's all the fookin' game isn't it, mate . . . all the fookin' game.'

*

I made the turn on the tight bend at the top of the canyon and gunned the car through the creaking gates. It still felt unreal, although Sylvio was evidently completely at home with it. Always moving forwards. I parked in the shade of the trees and we walked through the house, even more cavernous now in its emptiness, which was oppressive and isolating. We found Lana out on the deck, the high sun bouncing from the concrete. She was wearing a silver bikini even smaller than the one I'd last seen her in, her hair pulled back and her face free of make-up, something I rarely saw. She was far more beautiful this way. She and Sylvio hugged and kissed, un-embarrassed, and then she hugged me too, her back warmed by the sun. She smelled of fresh sweat, clean and deep, and vaguely of cigarettes. I wondered how it felt to be alone up here, in the overwhelming quiet.

We had a perfunctory interview, none of which I would use. Lana, like Sylvio, was far more interesting when she wasn't talking about music, and she was even less concerned by it. We sat out there for an hour or so to keep Marty happy and then Sylvio and I left. As we did, I glanced backwards towards the deck, and saw someone come out through the pool gate and stand next to Lana. It was Doug. He turned around and looked back into the house, but the light outside was too bright for him to see inside. I watched him for a moment and then turned to catch up with Sylvio.

*

Fast Eddie worked his magic on the rest of the record. Some bands paid many thousands of dollars to sound as cheap. Eddie made it sound like everyone else's – that was the point. Lana came in to do vocals and he threw us all out of the studio, even Sylvio and Tony, and coaxed a performance out of her, double-tracking her high, thin voice, hiding its weaknesses behind some clever arrangements, fading her under guitars, bringing her up when the moment suited her range. He mixed the whole thing down in the few remaining hours and we had a little playback party, the last notes ringing away just as the speed metal band pushed through the door for another smacked-out night. We carried on in the apartment in the

Marina, Eddie showing up with the sad-eyed girl from Lomita once he was sure that the speed metal band were high enough not to notice, or at least high enough not to care. I was wedged in a corner with Sylvio and Ray, me nursing a beer, them getting happily smashed. Across the room, I watched Iris talking to Marty. She had her back to me, her hair pulled into a ponytail that danced around her pale neck, and she wore a long skirt that covered her feet and touched the floor. She was holding a drink and making little hummingbird shifts from side to side, so that different parts of Marty kept appearing from behind her. Every now and again I caught the sound of her voice or her laugh. After a while, she must have sensed me looking at her because she turned around and gave a little wave. Later, unable to sleep, I held her in the dark.

Disappear here, my darling. Disappear here.

7. Matthew

Once, I went to Japan for an interview. It was a strange and alienating place of low skies and thin light where life seemed like an approximation of something familiar but with the details skewed and re-presented. Tokyo was a city of permanent dusk, of concrete and neon, its streets filled with indistinct faces and unreadable expressions. The gigs started at five or six in the evening and the crowds remained seated throughout. At the end of each song, they let out a high, hissing scream. The exhortations of the band – the usual stuff: 'Let's go fucking crazy', 'Come on, Tokyo, we're going to have some fun tonight' – were met with respectful applause. Later I was taken to a suite of rooms on the top floor of a towering city-centre hotel, its hushed luxury producing an ominous calm from everyone in it. The lift opened directly into the suite, where three of its external walls were made entirely of glass, offering giddying views. In the bedroom, on the emperor-sized bed, were two very young Japanese girls, each expressionless and mute. There were sex toys scattered across the floor. The band member I was there to see came out from the shower wearing a robe. His PR took me aside and said that if the piece I wrote mentioned the presence of the girls in any way, the magazine would never be granted another interview with the band, and seeing as they appeared on the cover three or four times per year, they were worth more to us than we were to them. He gave a perfunctory interview while we stared out of the windows (it was impossible not to, like watching a vast cinema screen, a sci-fi epic, a vista of infinite possibility), but there was nothing that he could say that told his story better than the place we found ourselves in. He had entered the third and final stage, where the answer to every question he ever had was yes, where nothing that could be done was left undone.

★

The memory of it came to me while I sat with Matthew at the Hollywood Roosevelt, out by the crumbling art deco glory of the courtyard pool where waiters hovered to serve the few of us there on a glowing afternoon. He had come to tell me his story, and I wanted to take him somewhere that we were unlikely to run into anyone I knew. Ray had turned me on to the Roosevelt. It was on Hollywood Boulevard, not far from Mann's, and it had once been *the* hotel in Los Angeles – the first Academy Awards were held at the Roosevelt, and Clark Gable had lived in a penthouse suite – but it had fallen out of fashion and now the Chateau and the Mondrian and the Sunset Marquis were the places to be seen in. The Roosevelt, with its cavernous interiors and filmic ghosts (it was allegedly the city's most haunted place, with its unexplained cold spots and its weeping spirits) had become a tourist curiosity. Yet it had genuine atmosphere (so rare here) and the drinks were cheap – a perfect, iced White Russian for a dollar. Ray had come along to take care of Donald, and although they hovered a few tables away, Ray's easy charm had soon engaged him and Matthew relaxed and began to talk.

★

He said he took Doc McGhee's pen in Doc McGhee's office and he signed the papers that Doc McGhee put in front of him. With Doc McGhee's pen, he signed his name over and over again, *Nikki Sixx, Nikki Sixx, Nikki Sixx* . . . His new name, his new life, the new life that he had dreamed of in LA, the life that he had imagined into existence when he took the Greyhound bus from Erie, Pennsylvania and slept in unlocked cars and nursed one beer all afternoon in the Troubadour Lounge until he met Mick Mars, and Mick Mars brought him here, to the offices of McGhee Entertainment, the offices where he left behind Matthew Trippe and became Nikki Sixx.

Mötley Crüe had an album called *Too Fast For Love* and they had gone on tour in Canada as support for a bigger act called Y&T. They weren't like Kiss or Van Halen or Ted Nugent, anyone famous, so it wasn't surprising that Matthew hadn't yet heard of them. They'd had – he would learn – a bass player called Nikki Sixx, who, according to Matthew, in the middle of 1983, crashed his Porsche on the freeway and did a pretty good job of fucking himself up (the list of injuries was extensive and debilitating, something about a shoulder, something about a hand), and now they needed another. He'd had to learn all about this other Nikki Sixx, everything about the guy, learn it and memorise it, because he was Nikki Sixx now. Born 11 December 1958 in San Jose, real name Frank Carlton Serafino Feranna (not 'Feranno', a lot of people got that wrong), grew up in Seattle with parents who were musicians, who in fact played with Frank Sinatra. Ran away from home at fifteen to go and stay with his grandparents on a farm in Twin Falls, Idaho, then moved on with his mother to Queen Anne Hill, Seattle, where he stole a Les Paul and formed a band. It was a pretty simple story to remember because it wasn't too far removed from the one he had lived.

Matthew knew how it felt to be Nikki Sixx even before he became him.

He didn't spend too long worrying about that, though. Instead he imagined the chicks, the trucks, the booze, the money . . . He went to live with Tommy Lee in a condo on Aryssa Avenue.

★

Matthew didn't know it, but Mötley Crüe had been running wild on the Strip for a couple of years. They'd lived in a cheap, walk-up two-bedroom apartment on North Clark Street, right by the Whisky a Go Go, all four of them plus a rolling cast of strippers, dancers and musicians, a party running permanently, the place quickly trashed, the doors kicked down, bottles smashed on the walls, piles of beer cans and fast-food containers piling up inside and out, rats on the patio, cockroaches in the oven, their lives, as Vince Neil would say, 'a blur of alcohol, drugs and sex', the depravity soon taking on an epic scale. Tommy had a girlfriend, nicknamed Bullwinkle by the rest of the band on account of her apparent resemblance to a cartoon moose, a girl whose jealous rages were the source of some of the worst fights seen in the house, but even though he was almost pathologically fucking any woman he came across, Tommy loved Bullwinkle almost as violently as she loved him. It was Bullwinkle who broke the plate-glass patio window with a fire extinguisher – it was never fixed, and soon the rats were inside the house as well as outside and the city authorities came around and issued an eviction notice that the band ignored and left pinned to the door.

Vince and Tommy were heavily into sex. Tommy was a romantic with a giant dick, Vince a classic narcissist for whom no amount of women was enough ('I've seen him fuck ten before a gig and another ten after,' said the band's first manager, Allan Coffman). Nikki liked to fuck too, but he liked drugs more. As for Mick, he was a strange cat, older than the others, and somewhat mysterious. Vince and Tommy were from LA. They'd barely had to move up the road to find the life that they wanted. It had been around them all along. They were born into it. Nikki and Mick had to make it happen in their own way. Nikki brought his dark nihilism, a pain that only heroin could extinguish. No other life awaited him. For Mick, the clock was ticking down. He'd been on the scene a long time. Behind him were the wife and three children, the many bar bands, the opportunities that had never come (Mick was not the only father in the band; Vince had a son too, born when he was seventeen).

Somehow the sheer chaos that they created had a force of its own; it drew people to them, pulled satellites into their orbit. Coffman found money, pressed a single, got some interest going. When he sold out, some guy from Canada came in (hence the tour up north, where no one knew who they were) and then after he'd gone, Doug Thaler, a booking agent who was a cousin of Ronnie James Dio, came in, and brought Doc McGhee with him. They'd sold 100,000 copies of *Too Fast for Love*, and an A&R man called Tom Zutaut signed them to Elektra Records (Vince responded by screwing Tom's girlfriend). They sold out every club in LA. Other bands copied how they looked, how they acted. Magazines began to write about them. They made videos that were shown on MTV. Beyond that, their sensibility chimed with the era. Punk was no one's idea of a good time any more. New Wave was for college kids. Radio rock was for middle America. In 1983 in Los Angeles, Mötley Crüe were for everyone else. The band may not have sensed it, but Doc McGhee did, and so did Elektra Records. Doc had instincts, he could smell it, taste it. Mötley Crüe was a way out for him, too, a way out from those ghost boats on the coast of Carolina, the safe houses full of drug money, a life that could only end one way. Doc would hold on as tight as the rest of them. Doc would not let his chance go. For those in the band and those outside it, for those who played in it and those who worked for it, for those who paid for tickets and bought the records, Mötley Crüe was a way to escape.

*

Matthew said that everyone called him Nikki. He got used to it. Mick told him that the other guy was still in the hospital. Matthew didn't think too much about it. After a week or so, Doc told him that he'd have to do some interviews. Matthew said they ran over the Nikki Sixx story again, and he remembered it all. He drank beer and got stoned. It made him more of an asshole, more like Nikki. It eased away his stammer, lit up a new part of his brain. The band were in the process of making a new album. Nikki had been the band's main writer, so Doc asked him to work on some of the songs. He said he wrote one called 'Danger', another called 'Knock 'Em Dead, Kid'. He shaped some of the others. They'd wanted to call the record *Shout With the Devil*, but Matthew suggested changing that to *Shout at the Devil*. He said he took the little pentagram that sometimes appeared on the band's flyers and turned it the other way around, the proper satanic way, with two points of the pentagram upwards. He knew what he was talking about. He'd been playing around with satanism for some years. At first it was just another way to rebel against the stultifying life in Erie, but for some reason he'd never dropped it. He began in the Church of Satan, which was a pretty infamous organisation founded by Anton LaVey, but now he'd moved onwards and upwards (or perhaps downwards) to the Temple of Set, a far more exclusive and secretive order of occultists run by Michael Aquino. Aquino had once been in the Church of Satan too, but he'd had philosophical disagreements with LaVey and founded the Temple via a magic ritual during the summer solstice of 1975. Aquino described the Temple as 'the intellectual wing of esoteric satanism'. Set, the deity at the head of the Temple, was not worshipped as a god, but instead was regarded as a role model for the adepts to follow as they rose up the pathway within the church. Aquino was said to be the highest grade of Setian. He was also a lieutenant colonel in the US Army. The Temple was said to have many powerful people amongst its members. Matthew knew Aquino well (he recited to me his telephone number from memory. It matched the one Donald would later give me). Matthew had a recurring dream where he'd sold his soul to the Devil. He tried various rituals. None of them worked. They left what he called 'scars'.

Doc had him rewrite some of the lyrics to the songs on *Shout at the Devil*. He said he helped Mick to arrange the music. He and Vince chanted 'JESUS IS SATAN' and ran it backwards underneath the title track. The album got done. Doc booked them onto a tour with Kiss. Before that, they made a video for a song called 'Looks That Kill'. Videos were the new thing to do. MTV had been going for three years, and it was becoming almost as good as radio play in breaking a band. On set he got into a fight with the director, this Italian guy called Marcelo. They'd been up since 4 a.m., and Marcelo had been giving him shit all day, so he'd said to Vince in a loud voice 'check out this Italian motherfucker'. They'd squared up, but then Doc stepped in because it was his money they were wasting. It had felt good though, it had felt like something that Nikki would have done. The record came out and immediately they got a load more shit from PMRC and the Christians because the album 'encouraged Satan worship'. He didn't care. He did worship Satan. The *Rolling Stone* review called them 'formulaic, innocuous and unoriginal'. The *Village Voice* said that *Shout at the Devil* was 'poor even by Heavy Metal's standards'. They went on tour with Kiss, and he finally got to meet his hero, Gene Simmons, who was a real cool guy and who never once raised his voice, no matter what happened. The day after the tour ended, Vince got dressed up in a US marine uniform and went out to a bar where he got in an altercation with a genuine female marine, who he punched in the face. *Shout at the Devil* shipped 1 million units and reached number seventeen on the Billboard charts. When Matthew went to stay with family in Florida for Christmas, he was in one of the biggest bands in America.

*

He went to Fort Myers. His mom was living there now. The whole family was coming for Christmas. He made sure that everyone he knew down there called him Nikki. On 11 January he took a plane to New York to start another leg of the tour, this time as support to Ozzy Osbourne. Kiss were big, but Ozzy was bigger. In 1984, Ozzy was the biggest and most controversial star in America. The combination of Ozzy and Mötley Crüe was a toxic one, and the tour quickly became an orgy of drug- and alcohol-fuelled madness. Ozzy was on prescription drugs as well as illegal ones. He was so out of it, he snorted a line of ants that were walking across the floor. He was essentially zombified by the scale of his drug intake. The tour got to Lakeland, Florida at the end of January, and a couple of shows were cancelled while Ozzy was briefly hospitalised after trying to eat a beer bottle.

Matthew had a friend called Cherry, more than a friend really, but Cherry was young – as in underage young. Sweet, though. Really sweet, and really hot. Cherry brought Matthew's car up from Fort Myers to Lakeland and they drove around together, just cruising, enjoying themselves. When they were driving back, he stopped to pick up a couple of hitch-hikers. He'd had to hitch himself, many times, so he liked to stop when he could. It turned out that the hitch-hikers were headed to Fort Myers too. Their names were Jeff and Chris, and they were cool guys, so cool that they carried on hanging out in Fort Myers until it was time for him to rejoin the Ozzy tour.

*

He knew that Ozzy didn't like him, he could feel it. He got angry, got wrecked, trashed a few hotel rooms, caused some mayhem of his own. The tour ended on 1 April 1984. Rich Fisher, who was the tour manager, came up to him and told him that he was going to be replaced by another Nikki Sixx. Frankie Feranna was coming back. He laughed it off. It was April Fools after all. He went back to Fort Myers. He had money in his pocket, not a fortune but a lot more than he'd had before. He was at his mom's house when Jeff called him.

'Hey,' he said. 'You remember Chris, right? Well, he's gonna have a drug party.'

He picked up Jeff and Chris, and they all got bombed. When they ran out of beer, Jeff went to borrow his car to get more, but he thought Jeff was too out of it to drive, so he took the three of them to the Pavilion shopping centre in Naples. While Jeff and Chris went to the liquor store, he visited the video shop where he used to buy magazines. He was talking to his friend Sam, who ran the bookstore nearby, when Chris comes jumping in front of Sam holding a knife to his throat. Sam lurched away in shock and Matthew just ran, ducking down behind a row of parked cars. Sam ran off to call the cops. Then Chris yells at him, 'Come on, Nikki,' and the three of them get back in his car and he drives as fast as he can until they're miles away. Jeff pulled out a pile of money and gave him a hundred bucks for driving. He had to admit, it was a hell of buzz. A few days later, they did it again. This time, Chris had a gun with him. That was a step way too far. He took off. He went to El Dorado, Arkansas, where Cherry lived. She stole some money from her father's wallet and they skipped town. They spent a few days in Jackson, Tennessee, and then he decided that they would head for his dad's hunting camp outside of Erie. No one would find them there. They switched cars somewhere in West Virginia. Now it was like something out of a movie he once saw, lovers on the run, making vows to one another, swearing their promises of for ever. They had the radio on, they sang along to the songs that she liked. They stopped at roadside diners and half-empty malls. He wondered if he had ever been happier. The things he had wanted had somehow come to him. As they drove east, he told her about this new life he had somehow imagined for himself.

They got to the hunting camp. After a couple of days, Jeff and a few other people showed up. They had a little party going, beer and pot. Fooling around, showing off for Cherry, he climbed up on the roof of the camp and jumped down. He broke his foot, had to go to the emergency room and have a cast put on it.

As that bone cracked, the thin new life that he had created did too. Jeff began to take his things, steal his beer, go joyriding in his car, light fires in the camp, and with the cast on his foot, there was nothing he could do to stop it, couldn't even fight him. Cherry got bored and homesick and spent her time bitching at him. Word got around the bars in town that Matthew Trippe was back, that he was claiming to be Nikki Sixx from Mötley Crüe.

Early one morning he woke Cherry and took her to the state police. He dropped her off outside the building and told her to go and tell them that she was a runaway and she wanted to go back home. She couldn't mention his name because he'd transported a minor across state lines. He watched her walk inside and then he drove into Erie to a friend he had there. She put him up for a few days but when he limped to the store one afternoon, the police picked him up.

He was questioned by two detectives. He tried to work out what it was they knew. They asked him if he was Matthew John Trippe. They asked him if he was Nikki Sixx. He refused to tell them. They ran both names through the computer. Nikki Sixx had a $50,000 bond against his name for an armed robbery in Naples, Florida. This one cop let him make a phone call. He rang the offices of McGhee Entertainment. Left a message for Doc. Doc never called. The detective told him that he could sit in jail in Erie, Pennsylvania for as long as it took, or he could sign Nikki Sixx's extradition papers and return to Florida to face the judge. He signed the papers. He rang Doc again and asked him to send a lawyer. No lawyer came. When he got up in court, he discovered that they'd made some sort of mistake with the paperwork and the judge had to release him on his own recognisance before trial. His stepfather allowed him to move back home to Fort Myers on the condition that he cut his hair and covered his tattoos. He got a job working at the Brown Derby. One day he picked up a magazine at the stand and read that Mötley Crüe had gone on tour in Europe as support to Iron Maiden. He called Doc and Doc told him that he now had a felony record and couldn't travel overseas, and you know, the show must go on. Doc told him to sit tight, and he'd soon be doing some promo work for *Shout at the Devil*. His trial date was set for 27 December. He asked Doc to send a lawyer. No lawyer came. On 8 December, Vince Neil, driving drunk to get beer for a party, crashed his car on the freeway in Los Angeles, killing his passenger, Nicholas Dingley, also known as Razzle, the drummer in a Finnish glam band called Hanoi Rocks, and badly injuring the occupants of a car travelling in the opposite direction. Vince was uninjured. He was taken to jail and charged with vehicular manslaughter. Someone came running up to Matthew in the street and told him that Vince was dead. Matthew laughed.

Matthew went to trial two months later. He was sentenced to two years' house arrest, six months of probation and a hundred hours of community service. Jeff got three years. Chris, who was the guy who had the knife and pulled the robbery, got off. It didn't seem right. Soon afterwards, he skipped town. He figured they'd never come to look for him in the place where he'd been caught, so he ran back to Erie. Pennsylvania was in the last grip of winter. When the cops came looking for him, he leapt out of a second-floor window down into the snow. He ran, but not too far. They put him

back in the county jail. This time he refused to sign the extra-
dition papers. He was in there with a bunch of thugs and
rapists. They'd all become Christians because they figured it
would help them get parole. It drove him crazy so he started
back with the Temple of Set, and when he did he discovered
that Mötley Crüe were beginning an American tour in Erie,
Pennsylvania.

★

For a long time he wondered why. Erie wasn't exactly a
rock 'n' roll town. Very few bands stopped off there. Finally
he figured that maybe they'd done it because they thought
that if they could pass Frankie Feranna off as Nikki Sixx in
Erie, they could do it anywhere. The tour had come and
gone by the time he got out of jail. He asked around town
for people who'd seen the show. A couple told him that
Frankie hadn't moved around much on stage. He didn't talk
or introduce the songs. The band had a new record out, too.
It was called *Theatre of Pain*. It had some of his songs on it,
he said. Doc had asked him to write a slow one and he'd
come up with 'You're All I Need'. The others hadn't liked it
so it went on the shelf. Now it was on *Theatre of Pain*. So
was another called 'Save Our Souls', which he'd originally
called 'Running Wild in the Night'. 'Hotter than Hell' was
on there, except now they were calling it 'Louder than Hell'.
There were other songs that the other guys had written but
that he'd been over and cleaned up, 'Black Widow', 'I Will
Survive', 'Red Hot'. The album sleeve still had the little
pentagram on, but there was a lot less of a satanic feel to
it. The band were wearing a lot less make-up and the clothes
were less leather and more glam.

He called up Doc McGhee. He told Doc he was running short of money. Doc told him that the royalties were starting to come in and that he would send him a cheque. The cheque never came. He bummed around Erie, Pennsylvania telling people his story. They didn't believe him. Word went around that he was a lunatic, a fantasist, a fraud. He got more and more into drugs to dull the pain of it all. He got out of shape and fat. He didn't look like Nikki Sixx any more. He drifted back to his family in Florida. They began to despair of him. He began to exaggerate his story. Now, he hadn't just joined Mötley Crüe after meeting Mick Mars in the Troubadour Lounge. Instead, he'd been the original Nikki Sixx. He'd formed Mötley Crüe. He'd written the songs and dressed the band and created their aesthetic and then he was thrown out by Doc McGhee. He was aware of how mad it all sounded coming from a fat guy with short hair who was living with his mom and stepdad in Fort Myers, Florida and still on house arrest, but he couldn't seem to stop himself from doing it. Then, according to Matthew, almost a year later, long after Vince Neil had somehow served just nineteen days in jail for killing Razzle and the band had toured America and *Theatre of Pain* had reached number six on the Billboard charts and become their biggest-selling record to date and the videos for the singles 'Home Sweet Home' and 'Smokin' in the Boys Room' had been on heavy rotation on MTV for months on end and the distance between him and them seemed unbridgeable, Mick Mars appeared out of nowhere and materialised in Fort Myers. He sent Clyde, who had been the band's lighting tech, to meet Matthew. He got pretty drunk before Clyde arrived and then followed him as he drove from Fort Myers to Safety Harbor. Clyde took them to a mall where he stopped to buy beer. As he waited for Clyde, Matthew fooled around in his car, pulling wheel spins in the parking lot. A patrol car saw him doing it and pulled over. He was still on probation, outside of his curfew area and drunk. Just as the cops were about to take him in, Mick Mars pulled up in a red rental car. He got out and spoke to the patrolmen, showed them something in his wallet and they waved him off. They drove back to a house somewhere and spent a couple of hours together. He said Mick told him about Vince's plea bargain and how they'd used the band's limited liability insurance to pay $2.6m in restitution by claiming that the party Vince and Razzle had just left had technically constituted 'a business meeting', about Tommy getting divorced and married again, and Frankie spending $3,000 a week on heroin. Mick told him that Doc got so pissed off with Vince getting drunk while he was on probation that he hired a couple of bouncers who were instructed to beat Vince up if he began drinking. Mick told him that Frankie had OD-ed at some chick's house and been hit with a baseball bat by a dealer trying to bring him around. How Tommy threatened to kill his new wife on their honeymoon. How Doc thought the band were essentially 'unmanageable'. Matthew asked Mick what he thought he should do. Mick said he didn't know, but he'd try to help him if he could.

*

The court ordered him to complete his probation in a rehab facility in West Palm Beach. The place was run by born-again Christians. JD, the programme director, told Matthew that he was not who he said he was. JD told Matthew's parents that he would sort him out. Matthew managed to call Michael

Aquino at the Temple of Set. Michael's wife called to speak to Nikki and JD told her that there was no one of that name at his facility. JD took all of the photographs of Mötley Crüe and the big book in which Matthew wrote down all of his dreams and stories and lyrics and had them destroyed. JD told Matthew that he was a fraud. By the time he left the clinic, his stammer was back and his hair was shorter than ever. He began going to bars and getting hammered. He told his story to anyone who would listen. No one believed him. He began getting into fights. His anger grew. It was Michael who told him what he should do: lose weight, grow his hair, stop talking, find a lawyer who could help him. When he looked like Nikki Sixx again, it was Michael who put him on to Donald.

Donald listened to his story. Unbeknown to Matthew he began to investigate it. For months, Donald played along when Matthew told him that he was the original Nikki Sixx, that he formed the band, that he wrote all of the songs and appeared in all of the videos. Then one day, out of the blue, Donald had asked him, 'So when are you going to come clean?' Donald had found the court documents in which Frank Feranna had legally changed his name to Nikki Sixx back in 1980. He had videotapes of television interviews in which the person introduced as Nikki Sixx was clearly not Matthew John Trippe. He had publishing credits from the Recording Industry Association of America that showed some of the songs that Matthew claimed to have written were in fact by other members of the band. He had lists of tour dates that Matthew could not physically have been present for according to court papers, passport records and registers of state taxpayers.

Matthew asked Donald why he hadn't just thrown him out

when he had found them, why he hadn't dismissed him as a fantasist and a fraud as the police and the courts and JD and all of the people he'd fought with in bars and nightclubs had done. Donald showed him some other evidence too. A statement from a reporter on a Pittsburgh newspaper who said he recognised Matthew's voice as that of the Nikki Sixx he had once interviewed. Some photographs in the *Theatre of Pain* tour book that seemed to show Nikki Sixx almost the same height as Vince Neil instead of towering over him as he had in earlier videos and images. A Japanese magazine picture of Nikki Sixx half naked in a shower with physical characteristics that apparently matched those of Matthew Trippe and not Frank Feranna. The tape of an MTV interview with Vince and Nikki in which Nikki Sixx wore full make-up and said very little. Background material on the criminal history of Doc McGhee.

'So,' Donald had said to him. 'Tell me what happened.'

He did then, everything he said he could remember from the moment he met Mick Mars to the day that Rich Fisher told him that he was to be replaced by another Nikki Sixx. He told Donald about the Temple of Set too, even though Donald was a born-again Christian himself. One day they'd been in the office and Donald had taken a call from someone who identified themselves as 'Matthew Trippe from Arista Records'. Donald had been taken aback but Matthew recognised the voice as that of Mick Mars. He remembered Mick telling him that he would help him if ever he was able to.

*

When he looked up and said, 'And yeah, well, that's kind of it. That's my story,' I realised that the rest of the room had telescoped away, that I'd been listening to Matthew Trippe and his strange, lulling voice for almost two hours, and all the while running through my head had been this song that was on heavy rotation on MTV with a chorus that said 'What I want/Is to be forgiven'.

Matthew's voice, so distinctive in the way he'd been taught to almost sing the words that he began to stammer, elongating them until he could finish pronouncing them, was just one of the many questions about what he had said, so many that I wasn't entirely sure where to start. I decided not to, at least not there, as the last of the woozy afternoon ran away from us in the bar of the Hollywood Roosevelt hotel. Donald and Ray came and joined us. We drank more beers. Donald began talking excitedly about something he called 'the marijuana experiments', which he claimed would go some way to helping the case – he'd met a speech therapist who recommended pure medical dope that he had somehow managed to obtain and had given to Matthew under strict conditions and that had, he said, gone some way towards eradicating his stammer. 'He talks that way because his brain moves too quickly,' Donald said. 'Psychotropic drugs slow the brain down, and I'm telling you, man, when Matt smoked that stuff he sounded like you and me . . .'

'I was fucking stoned a lot when I was with Crüe,' Matthew said.

'We just gotta be careful,' Donald went on. 'He's been an addict, been in rehab.' He patted Matthew's shoulder. 'We gotta keep you clean, bud.'

'More's the pity,' Matthew said. I waited for him to laugh, but he just stared at his beer.

*

Iris arrived a little later to pick us up. She smirked at Donald, who regarded her suspiciously. Matthew stared at her legs, his head nodding forwards drunkenly (another beer had tipped him over the edge).

'Wow,' Iris said. 'You do look like him . . .'

I'd forgotten that Iris hadn't yet seen Matthew in the flesh. I introduced them.

'Cool,' Matthew said. 'Hey honey. Where we going tonight?'

'You're not really Nikki Sixx, you know . . .'

I laughed. So did Ray. Iris had some good lines in her. Donald glowered. Matthew said nothing more.

'Well, that was weird,' Iris said, once Ray and I were crammed into her little car. 'Donald creeps me out.'

'There is something odd about him,' Ray said.

'Let's face it, there's something odd about them both,' she said. 'They're quite hard to take seriously.'

'I think that's the genius of the whole thing,' I said. 'If I was Doc McGhee, and I really was going to pull a stunt like this, Matthew is exactly the kind of person I'd do it with. He can't get his story straight. He'll pretty much do anything anyone tells him to do. He fucks up all the time. He has no credibility.'

'Yeah . . .' said Iris. 'Or he may have no credibility because the whole story is a crock . . . Do you really believe him?'

'That's the point, I suppose. Seventy per cent of everything he says sounds like bullshit. And then he comes out with a detail that he just couldn't know unless he'd been there, and you think, "Oh, okay . . ." I guess it's like Marty says, they don't need to win, they just need to be convincing enough for Doc to settle with them.'

'Donald told me he doesn't care about the money any more,' said Ray, and smiled.

'That's right.' I said. 'And Matthew's really anxious to start living in his car again.'

★

We swung by the Hyatt. Iris took a shower while Ray and I sat in the bar, where the singer with the sad voice was back again, and after the weeks in the studio while Lana made her record, she sounded strong and pure, her eyes closed as she sang – something about a place beyond the sea, a lover on golden sands . . . For a moment she was transported, no longer caring that she was in an almost empty hotel bar in the early evening. Ray and I stopped talking and watched her. When the song finished there was a moment of silence and then we began applauding. She smiled and announced that the band were taking a break. She walked over to the bar, where the bartender had a tall drink waiting. She pulled up a stool next to Ray. In a hotel bar in Delaware or Kalamazoo she would have turned heads, had every eye on her, but this was LA. Ray introduced himself. They clinked their glasses together. Her name was Stella, and she'd once almost had a deal with Capitol Records. Now she sang here and at a place up in Malibu and she tried out for background work in movies, films that had bar scenes with singers in them.

'Never give up, huh,' she said, and sipped at her drink.

Iris came down. Ray introduced her to Stella.

'Where are you guys going?' Stella asked.

'Party,' said Iris.

'Are we?'

'Mmm hmmm . . .'

'I think I'm going to stick around here, listen to some music,' Ray said. Stella smiled at him.

It was good to be alone with Iris. I slipped my hand on to her leg as she drove. She felt good, looked good, smelled good.

'So . . .' I said.

'So . . .'

'So . . . Where are we going then?'

'Well . . . uh . . . okay, Blair rang yesterday . . .'

'Blair . . .'

'Yeah.' Iris composed herself. 'She called the office. And you know, after what's been happening with us, I thought, I can't be scared my whole life. I don't want to feel that way.'

I took my hand from her leg and held her hand. I felt a great tenderness for her.

'So . . .'

'So there's a screening of her father's film, and then there's a party. I have no real idea why she asked, but she has. So . . . That's the so . . .'

'Okay then, but if she wants me to jerk off with her I'm probably going to do it this time.'

'You asshole,' Iris said. She laughed and squeezed my hand. Her eyes were filmy, maybe from the breeze and maybe not. 'Thanks . . .' she said.

We were silent for a moment.

'It was nothing.'

'You really are an asshole, aren't you . . .' This time she punched my arm. I slid my hand back on to her leg as she gunned the little car along the Hollywood Freeway.

★

The screening was on the Paramount lot, just another event in my life that should have seemed extraordinary yet somehow didn't any more. Iris drove us under the grand white gates. We passed sound stages and great empty hangars, following the signs on private roads until we found the screening room. We bypassed the line of people outside and we were given drinks and shown through the dark to big leather seats. The room already seemed full but then the queues from outside came in too, Iris explaining that they were there to test the movie so that the studio could discover whether the public liked it or not, but given that they were probably all out-of-work actors and writers it was like sticking your record on at the Tropicana and seeing if people danced. The film was the same one that we'd watched on videotape at Blair's father's house, but Iris didn't seem to remember. I thought of her and Blair dancing drunkenly together to the songs on the soundtrack, shouting the choruses at one another, Iris falling asleep before the thing finished. This time we watched in silence, the saturated colours from the giant screen bleeding into the darkness, illuminating Iris in washes of light and flickering shadow. Afterwards, we were handed passes to the party – 'A night of lights and magic' – and shown to a fleet of cars lined up outside, Iris and I soon sunk into the hushed luxury of one as it purred from Hollywood up into the hills, the engine audible only as a deep-throated whirr as it climbed the hairpins, Iris with her head tucked into my shoulder, both of us drinking beers from the cooler placed inside the car. It took us up the steep climb to the observatory in slow procession with the other limos, finally swinging into a car park, where a valet grabbed the door and ushered us out and towards the deck, where, in the twilight of early autumn, the great basin below us glowed. Iris gave an involuntary shiver – the breeze up in the canyon was chilly, but it wasn't just that, it was the atmosphere of the place. Iris had spent most her life here and she still felt it, a liminal sense of loneliness and isolation that seemed ever-present if sometimes hidden.

Iris barely knew anyone at the party – she smiled at a couple of girls, perhaps more of Blair's crew from their schooldays, but I didn't ask and she didn't say. I took more beer from the circling waiter, wondering idly for a moment what we would do about Iris's car before remembering again that in LA, nothing like that was ever a problem: the movie company's car would take us home and then Iris could simply call another from her work account or from her father's to take her back to the studio when she needed to collect her car. It was part of the echelon she was in, that all of these people were in, a zone where the usual problems simply weren't problems and something else had to take their place.

We sat opposite one another under an old palm, Iris's feet resting on my chair, her long pale legs shining in the lights that were hanging from the trees all around us, and from time to time I reached forward and took one of her soft calves in my hand and held it gently, feeling the weight of the muscle and the smoothness of her skin. I squeezed it gently and she closed her eyes and rolled her head on her neck.

'This is nice, she said. 'I'm glad we did this. Even though we'll have to get back in there . . .'

She gestured towards the massing bodies coming together at the centre of the observatory platform. There were perhaps a hundred people now, their noise and clamour growing steadily, their shouts and laughs becoming more raucous as the milling waiters shared around their ever-filling trays. I watched a gorgeous, aloof actress resist the advances of a guy in a tuxedo jacket and jeans, him only backing off when an older, richer, unsmiling man came over and took her hand. I watched her ass sway as she disappeared back into the party.

'That was Blair's father,' Iris murmured, and I realised that she'd been watching too. 'He looks exactly the same as he used to. He must have had some work done . . . He's fucking frozen in time . . .'

She seemed a little like someone standing on the edge of a swimming pool, afraid to make her first dive. She had to jump in a minute or she might not at all.

'Come on,' I said, and pulled her to her feet. 'Let's get in there.' I held her hand and pulled her towards the throng. There was an odd atmosphere, the party had none of the rage of the music-business ones I was used to, where desperation, hunger and neediness drove a weird kind of abandonment, an uninhibited wildness that meant almost anything could happen. In its place there was a deadening cool designed to signal that this was normal, humdrum, everyday. Blair shimmered towards us, kissed Iris hello and dragged her by the hand towards a group of girls standing at the bar. As she did, she turned around and gave a little wave. I watched as the girls hugged Iris in turn, their faces masks of fake surprise. Iris seemed okay with it. I hoped so.

I took a drink from one of the circling waiters, a young, handsome guy with a deep tan and electrically white teeth accentuated by the lighting that was now bathing the deck.

'Hey, enjoy the movie?' he asked.

'Yeah, it was alright, I guess.'

'I was up for a part,' he said. 'Eric . . . you know, the guy who gets high at the party and almost drowns in the pool?'

I remembered the scene, but only because I'd just seen the film. It had been over in less than a minute.

'I got down to the second read but then they went another way, I guess.'

'That's bad luck. I'm sure you could have done it.' (This was a non-controversial statement. I could have done it. 'Eric' didn't have to do much more than look stoned and gurgle.)

'Thanks, man, I'm sure I could. So, you in the business? You know anyone on the movie?'

'Not really. I'm just here with my girlfriend. She's a friend of the producer's daughter.'

'Cool thing. What's her name?'

'My girlfriend, or the producer's daughter?'

He smiled again. 'I'm not hitting on your girlfriend, bro. Just trying to catch a break, you know.'

'I know. Her name's Blair. That's her right there.' I gestured towards the bar, where Blair was openly flirting with a hawkish-looking guy wearing a silk scarf over his shirt. She swayed in front of him, her head tilted to one side, her body close to his. He paid her scant attention, constantly looking away to scout the room.

'She's hot,' he said almost to himself. 'Hey, who's the guy she's with?'

'I have no idea,' I said (although I did: I was pretty sure it would turn out to be her dealer).

'Cool. So want to come around the back and smoke a joint?'

I followed him across the patio, beyond the bar and behind a catering tent where several of the waiters were standing about, passing around a diminishing stub. We joined them. Each time the joint reached me I passed it along without a toke.

'Hey, don't you . . .'

'No, I don't like it.'

'Cool, bro. Neither do I really. It eases the pain of nights like tonight though.' He laughed. 'It's just boring, dude. You have to smile so much.'

'And eat too much shit from other people,' said one of the others.

'Yeah, serious shit. The worst is when you have to hand a drink to some guy that you've seen at a hundred open calls and you know he's not as good as you, he's just sucked some other guy's dick to get the gig . . .'

'Like the fuckin' dude in there . . .' Another of the waiters, chiselled, blond, movie-star handsome, gestured beyond the tent. 'I know for a fact that's what he's done . . .'

'And you don't, right?'

'Naah. Well . . . Only for a second lead, minimum . . .'

'Dude, you'd do it for a credit . . .'

'I heard he'd do it for an advert . . .'

'Man, he did it to get here tonight . . .'

They broke up laughing, the dope already having an effect. They leaned forwards as they smoked and wafted their hands in the air, trying to avoid the smoke attaching itself to their clothes. They reminded me of the kids in bands on the Strip, hanging around, handing out flyers, laughing and joking and wondering why the world was opening up for other people and not for them. I wondered that too, as we stood there within touching distance of the men and women who held the key. They were good-looking guys, they had poise and humour. To an outsider like me, they were no different to the cast of the movie who drifted around the party.

I told them about the sexy vampire waitress who Marty had hired. I still had the card in my pocket. I pulled it out and passed it around.

'Hey, yeah, cool, we know her. That's Laura, right? Dark-haired girl. She's hot, man.'

'She said she'd sleep with me for a hundred dollars . . .'

'And you know what – you'd have had a good time, too.'

★

We hung around behind the tent until the music got louder and the lights across the deck went down and the atmosphere became charged and the waiters had to return to work. The queues for the restrooms grew. I looked around for Iris but couldn't find her. I drifted for a while before I ran into the guy I'd seen Blair flirting with. I asked him where she was, and he simply nodded towards the restrooms. I grabbed another beer, drifted around some more, spoke to people I didn't know (not something I usually had the nerve to do), and before I knew it, something like hours had passed and when I went to take a piss I felt someone tug at my arm and when I turned around I saw Blair, her hair bedraggled, her face bone-white, the pupils of her eyes like two sharp bright pins.

'I am really wrecked,' she said. 'Can you help me because I'm kind of scared. This coke is cut with speed. I fucking hate speed, it freaks me right out, so can you just help me because I keep thinking something bad is going to happen . . .'

'Sure. What do you want me to do?'

'Talk to me . . . Do you have any dope?'

'No, I don't. Some of the waiters do.'

She thought for a moment. 'Do you have any Xanax? Or Vicodin. Do you have any Vicodin?'

'You know I don't, Blair. I'm not the guy for that.'

She ignored me. 'Because I just need to take the edge off this FUCKING SPEED . . .' A few people looked around. 'It's making me grind my teeth. It's making my skin itch.' She raked her nails along her arms, raising sharp red weals in the flesh. I took her hand and told her to stop.

'Just relax, it's okay. It'll stop if you don't scratch it. It'll all pass soon. Tell me about that guy I saw you with earlier. Was that Mark? Did he give you this?'

'Yes, that's him, the asshole. He says this is the best he has, but I know that's bullshit. This is LA.'

She tried to scratch herself again. She pulled her hand free from mine and grabbed at her nose, squeezing it hard. 'Christ,' she said.

'It's okay,' I said again. 'It'll pass. Tell me about some of the people here. Where are the girls that you were with?'

'What girls?' She still seemed angry and distracted.

'The girls that you and Iris were with when we got here.'

'I don't remember.' She stared hard over my shoulder. 'I don't know who you're talking about. I just need to find someone who has some Xanax . . .'

She pushed past me quite suddenly. I followed her but there was a growing crush around us and she slipped away. I made a slow circuit of the party, pushing through groups and couples, fielding harsh looks from people who thought that I was trying to jump the long queues for the bar and the ever-lengthening line for the restrooms. Iris was nowhere to be found. The music had become oppressively loud now, the low-level lighting of earlier had given way to harshly coloured gels that pulsed with the beat. At the wall by the platform edge, some giant arc lights swung white beams out over the canyon, where they were soon enveloped by the darkness. On the hillside above, an illuminated sign picked out the name of Blair's father's film. I stared at it for too long and it burned itself on to my retinas.

After a while I realised that Iris must have left. I stood at the edge of the platform. I could feel the heat of the great arc light nearby. There were some other refugees here, seeking respite from the noise and the light. The beer rush I had became a more drunken wooziness – a sheet of glass between me and reality. I didn't know if it felt good or bad. I nursed another beer anyway, some increasingly maudlin and scary scenarios about what might have happened to Iris coming into my mind: *Iris getting drunk and leaving with girls she barely knew; Iris getting drunk and leaving with a guy they'd introduced her to; Iris getting drunk and being persuaded into the back of a stranger's car; Iris drunk and horny and not quite in control, stumbling around an apartment she did not know; Iris suddenly alone and disorientated, left by the side of a road in the dark of the canyon . . .*

I felt a kind of distant and lurid dread, dulled by the glass between me and the world. I drifted back into the party, where, a little later, I thought I caught sight of her, just the back of a leg, the curve of her spine, a familiarity of movement before she was gone into the crowd (I have wondered many times since whether that was her, but the pulsing lights, the crush, the disorientating noise, the screen between me and the world made it impossible to be sure). Time became an abstracted, hazy thing. I'm not sure how long it took me to finish more beer, write down the name and number of the waiter (false promises of a meeting that would never be arranged, an intro- duction to Blair's father that would not happen), a final encounter with Blair, calmer now but in animated conversation with a group I didn't recognise, and then to a queue that was being ushered into the gleaming limousines that began their procession down the hillside, winding into the black hills and then the lights of West Hollywood, the driver talking to me about all of the auditions he'd had, the traffic on Sunset, the trees lining the road, Iris's place coming into view, the car slowing, the door opening, the driver offering a card, the hush of night around the large houses, another evening coming to its end.

★

I stepped out of the car. The air felt intoxicatingly cool. I stood on the path for a moment and breathed it in. I heard the limo drive off. The palms creaked in the wind as my head swam in the darkness. I thought I saw birds flying overhead, their wings rushing, black shapes against the black sky. I was, I conceded, pretty wrecked. The screen of glass was still there, separating me. I walked up the path, got the door open and went inside. The place felt empty, the rooms dark, absence suggesting itself. Somehow I knew that Iris wasn't here.

I came to the lounge at the rear of the house and slumped on to the sofa, and I must have been there for several minutes before I found I was not alone.

'Hey you,' said Brenna, who was curled in her armchair, her robe wrapped around her, a book at her feet. 'You woke me. Where have you been? Where is my Iris?'

I gave her a brief precis of the evening: the party, Blair, losing Iris and not being able to find her again.

'Don't worry,' she said. 'It's only a party . . . She's been to hundreds.'

'You're right.' I realised how ridiculous I sounded. 'I'm quite drunk.'

'Well, you know what you should do. Have another.'

I saw that she had a bottle of wine, half drunk, by the side of her chair. She got up and walked across the room to get a glass, bare legs, bare feet, painted nails, her steps whispering on the wooden floor. She sat back down and poured me a glass, her leg sliding through the split in her robe. She looked at me looking at her. She waited a moment before flicking the robe closed.

'Cheers,' she said, in a horribly fake English accent.

'Bums up.' The wine was warm in my throat. It hit me with a rush that I wasn't expecting. The maudlin feeling began to lift with it.

'So, Blair was there?'

'Yeah, out of her head on bad coke.'

Brenna snorted. 'Well who isn't? It's too easy here. You grow up with it.'

'But you . . .'

'I had my moments,' she said. 'My life was . . . Well, let's not go there. Why would I tell you? I've not made my mind up about you yet.'

'In what way?'

'In every way.'

She had that odd little enigmatic smile on her face, one I'd seen before. We drank for a while longer and my mind began to reach – I knew that the opposite was happening, the alcohol was shutting sections of it down, but that wasn't how it felt. It could be a beautiful and elusive thing, like a glide down a previously hidden path. Brenna seemed to loosen up too. She began talking about movies that she liked, how she couldn't watch those that featured people whose bodies she'd waxed or bleached.

'Too much reality,' she said. 'Once I've seen their ass six feet high, it's over for me. Sometimes I can tell it's not even them. It's an ass double or a different pair of tits . . .'

She drained her glass, told more stories: the actress who left her tampon in while Brenna waxed her pubic hair, the studio executives who rolled over with hard-ons. The only clients she really liked were the strippers and the porn stars, dulled by so much intimacy.

'One guy always says to me, "You're the only person I know who sees as much pussy as I do . . ."'

'What a life you lead . . .'

She smirked. 'I know,' she said. 'Let's have music.' She got up and fiddled with the stereo. Rick Springfield came on – 'Jessie's Girl' (a song I can never hear without thinking of that night, and how deliberately she chose it). Brenna began to dance, mouthing the words as she did.

She pulled me to my feet, hung her arms around my neck, sang softly in my ear. All of that body swelled against me.

'We're not really going to do this are we?'

We kissed. I wasn't sure who'd started it. She broke away.

'You've wanted this since you saw me in the bedroom, haven't you?' she said.

We kissed again. It was unstoppable now, whatever it was, whatever wreckage it brought. She opened her robe and I slid my arms inside it.

It was unfamiliar, clumsy, hurried, carnal. Iris there on the edge of my thoughts.

The one thing your lover can't give you – the experience of another.

Afterwards she lay back on the couch, propping her head on one hand. She stroked my shoulder with the other. The Rick Springfield tape turned itself over. The lamp in the corner of the room kept us half in shadow. The air was cool. I shivered.

'Are you feeling cold or guilty?' Brenna said, running her hand over my goosebumps.

'Well, both, I suppose.'

'So you should . . .'

Her face, expressionless. She kissed me again, hard, so hard our teeth clicked together.

'I've made my mind up about you,' she said. 'You're just like all the rest, aren't you?'

'Am I?'

'Yes, you fucking are. Right now, you're thinking, "Iris could come through that door at any moment . . ."'

She was right, I was. The buzzing, drunken high was gone too, and the hangover was back, woozy and sour.

'Don't worry,' she said. 'I'm not going to say anything. I love her, I won't hurt her.'

'What the fuck were you doing then?' I regretted the words as soon as they were out of my mouth. It was fear more than anything, fear and shame, but it sounded like something else.

Her eyes were hard and cold now. She pushed me away, stood up, pulled on her robe.

'I'm sorry,' I said. 'I didn't mean that. Look, we . . . I fucked up. It's not you. I just . . . I really like her . . . I don't know what I was doing.'

She smiled.

'That didn't sound great either, did it . . .'

She let me hold her for a moment. Her head was bowed. She pulled away. 'I'm going to bed,' she said. 'Just don't fuck her around.'

'I won't . . .'

'Forgive me if I don't believe that.'

She walked out, closing the door behind her. I got dressed and lay back on the couch. The ceiling swam. I closed my eyes, lay still for a while and the next thing I remembered was waking in a sun-filled room, too warm, dry-mouthed and with a thin headache, to Iris standing over me, smiling cheerily.

'Oh dear,' she said. 'What's happened to you . . . ?'

*

I stared up at her, framed in the bright blades of light, dust motes circling around her, her hair on her shoulders. She was fresh, beautiful, a creature of the morning not the dark. I could barely look at her. I had a swell of panic in my stomach, a coward's response. The night with Brenna felt like it was surrounding us, readable on my face.

'Oh God, sorry, Iris, I . . .'

She knelt down next to me, put a cool hand on my forehead. She smelled clean, pure. Her eyes shone. If she had seen Brenna, Brenna had evidently said nothing to her.

'Come on,' she said. 'Shower and breakfast.' As she got back up her heel caught the empty wine bottle that Brenna had left by the sofa. It clattered on the floorboards.

'Had a big night, did you? Drinking alone is never good . . .'

I groaned and sat up.

'Yeah, well . . .' I caught a waft from my clothes, stale and slept-in, an undernote of booze and someone's perfume. I felt the panic rise again, and slipped quickly past Iris and towards the bathroom.

I showered and dressed, and while Iris cooked eggs in the kitchen I cleared up in the lounge room, got rid of the bottle and the glasses, checked under the cushions for underwear or anything else that might incriminate me. I was pretty sure Brenna hadn't been wearing anything under her robe – I had a hazy vision of me pushing it from her shoulders, a memory that brought a sharp, shocking pang of excitement. I tried to shove it away.

'*You've wanted this since you saw me in the bedroom . . .*'

Her voice, her words.

'*Yes I did . . . I have . . .*' Words I had whispered in her ear.

Iris set down the food and filled me in on what had happened to her. She'd seen Blair too ('Off her face. She told me her nose had been bleeding. She really is a fuck-up . . .') but only briefly before she'd slipped away with a couple of her old school friends for some drinks back in West Hollywood and ending up at the Chateau for nightcaps from where they'd shared a cab that did the rounds of their houses, with Iris as the last drop (my luck really had been in) and when she'd come in I was out for the count on the couch, offering no response to her as she'd tried to wake me, so she had gone to bed alone.

'You keep missing out,' she said, and grinned, her sweetness bringing another pang, this time of shame (I'd managed a hopefully convincing smile in return, and Brenna had appeared briefly in the doorway, wearing a business suit, her hair pulled severely back. 'Farewell, lovebirds,' she'd said, and given me a neutral stare before she turned and left).

★

Iris called a car to take her to her office. She handed me her keys and asked if I would go and collect her little red car from the studios. Once there, I decided to abandon any plans of writing and drive out to the Marina and find Sylvio. It was a perfect late summer's day, the light golden and flooding down. The whitewashed walls of the great hangars at the film studio shimmered in it, their hard edges abutting the sea-blue sky. I slid into the driver's seat of Iris's car, the smell of her perfume on the seat belt, the interior warmed by the sun. For the first time I felt the intimations of something better in the day. On the taxi ride out, I'd been running through a series of increasingly lurid scenarios in which Iris had discovered what had happened and I'd imagined my responses: flat-out denial (probably unworkable given her and Brenna's closeness – Iris would know); claims of overwhelming drunkenness ('I don't even remember it happening – there must have been something in my drink' – that didn't explain Brenna's actions, though, or how I'd managed to go through with it); mistaken identity ('I'd fallen asleep there, someone was there and I thought it was you . . .' – Iris would really have to want to believe that one, and again it didn't explain Brenna). I even briefly considered some sort of blackmail or baroque and persuasive story from Brenna ('She told me that you'd asked her to do it, it was a thing that you two had . . .' – a notion that would, admittedly, sound more likely in a porn flick than anything that ever happened to me). Then there was an admission, the truth, but I genuinely found it unbearable to contemplate how her face would look as I told her.

Ultimately I knew none of them would play out. I would just say nothing, and hope that Brenna didn't either. The knowledge would be my penance, and I could feel its weight. It was a punishment of sorts, something that would take time to dissipate, and while it did, it would always have a hold.

The morning traffic was slow on Venice Boulevard, only easing for the last couple of miles out to the ocean, where the breeze was up and the first few wisps of cloud were visible in the blue. I parked in the Marina and walked to Sylvio's apartment. There was no answer to the buzzer, but as I walked down the steps back into the street I saw him crossing the road, a coffee in his hand.

'Brother!' he shouted and raised a fist above his head as he walked. It was another of his signature moves; he'd cribbed it from a video he'd seen of a boxer called Roberto Durán. Sylvio loved Durán, and often told long anecdotes about him taken from a biography of Durán but related as if Sylvio had been there. His favourite, which I'd heard many times, was about Durán knocking out a horse for a bet. He gave me a long hug. We walked back through the Marina to the coffee shop. He said that Marty had been driving him crazy about Lana's album. He wasn't sure about the mastering, didn't like the ideas for the cover.

'He's got Ray back at the house today. They're doing more pictures. It's supposed to be printing tomorrow . . .' He sighed. 'Not even Ray can shoot that many variations of a chick with her tits hanging out. He wants me up there again, but you know, fook that . . .' Sylvio had a pragmatic attitude to his sister's sexual allure, but I guessed there were some things he didn't want to see.

'Want to go to Malibu instead?' I asked.

'Now that's more fookin' like it . . .'

I got the car on to the Pacific Coast Highway, the great ocean to one side of us, the Palisades looming up on the other, the names on the exit signs bringing more thoughts of Iris. We passed the place where we'd had breakfast after the night at Blair's. I remembered how she'd looked in that little café, pale and trembling, laying herself bare. We passed the little shack where we'd eaten that evening, too, watching the distant lights on the tip of Catalina. The regret was sharp, the past refracted through it and irrevocably changed. Something pure had gone. That was my burden.

'I fucked Brenna last night.'

Sylvio actually looked shocked. He put his head back and laughed at me. 'Fookin' hell,' he said. 'Did you? I wouldn't mind that myself . . . What was it like?'

'I can't really remember.'

'Yeah, right . . .'

'Well . . . not much.'

'No one would forget those tits . . .'

'Jesus . . .'

'Fookin' hell, relax. What's the matter?'

'Iris . . .'

'Well, I wouldn't fookin' tell her for a start.'

'I wasn't planning to.'

'You're alright then, aren't you. There's only one other person knows, and if she says anything you just deny it.'

I didn't reply.

'Listen,' he said. 'Sylvio's lesson – people believe what they want to believe. You just have to give them the chance to believe it.'

It worked for him, I knew that. I'd seen him do it, and more than that, I'd watched him become the character he'd created for himself. He dressed like a rock star, talked like one, behaved like one, took his cues from the rock stars that he had wanted to be, and well, here he was. For all that people had laughed at him, dismissed him, ridiculed him, he had simply stood in the face of it all and denied what they had said. And now he was in LA, in a band, with a record out. He was a force. As we drove he described some of his many close encounters with women – women and their boyfriends, women and his other women. I'd seen some of them too, seen his schtick, turning up at their houses with a bottle of champagne and a bottle of Mateus Rosé, a combination that he claimed never failed; his furtive encounters on tour buses and in venue back rooms; his affair with the girlfriend of a guy who was once his manager (I'd seen some of that, on tour somewhere in England, the manager, an amiable day-jobber called Dickie arriving at soundcheck asking 'Where's Rachel? Where's Sylvio?', Sylvio swaggering in a few minutes later practically still doing up his trousers and walking straight over to give Dickie the usual hug).

I just didn't have that in me.

'Hey,' he said, 'it's a good problem to have, isn't it – "All these American chicks want to sleep with me and let me stay in their houses and drive their cars. Boo fookin' hoo . . . When will it stop?"'

I laughed at him. He was ridiculous, but maybe he was right as well. Perhaps I could will myself into his way of thinking. First act it and then become it . . .

'This isn't bad, is it,' he said, and put his feet up on the dash the way Iris often did. 'A couple of English lads on their way to the 'Bu in a flashy car. Hope all of those fookers back at the magazine office are having a good day . . .'

He pulled his sunglasses from his forehead and over his eyes as he closed them, occasionally mouthing along to the songs on the radio as I steered Iris's little car off the freeway and up into the bluffs.

We walked out across the headland, high on the rocky pathways just outside the colony, the sky over the ocean cloud-less and vast and dissolving into a big-screen haze at the horizon. Sylvio went ahead, the cliff dropping down towards the town. He stood below me, looking like a rock star in a video clip. The wind blew his hair around. He gazed out over this panorama. I wondered if he was hearing music that he was going to write: that was in him somewhere, along with everything else. Beneath him on the long white beach the movie star houses nestled in their crags, their decks jutting out on to the sand. The whole place looked as though it could vanish into the ocean at any moment.

'Disappear here . . .' You could, too, if you had a few million dollars.

The night I'd spent at Iris's father's place further along the coast . . . he and Iris serving us food, Iris asleep beside me in the little guest house, turned on her side and breathing softly, the pale ladder of ribs under my palm. The weight of the sea behind us. I felt another little pang for Iris. Sylvio turned around and looked up at me. He mimed playing a guitar. He pulled his Carlos Santana face. He looked epic and ridiculous. We followed the path down the bluffs and into the colony and ate lunch in a little café talking about the records he was going to make, the books I was going to write. This was what he was really good at: making people feel good, imagining a future that, while we talked about it in the Malibu sunlight, felt inevitable.

*

We drove back along the coast, through LA and towards the hills. On Wilshire we caught three sets of lights, and each time the same convertible pulled up alongside us. Two girls were in it, both tanned, both in shades, one blonde, one dark, their radio turned up and playing 'Round and Round', this song by Ratt that seemed to be on permanent heavy rotation in LA all through the summer. Sylvio leaned over to them and started singing. At first they ignored him, but by the second light they were sneaking looks and by the third he was telling them to follow us, which they did until we reached

Sunset. He waved as we took the exit, and the blonde girl waved back.

'Chicks, man,' he said to no one in particular.

Up at Marty's house, Ray had Lana sitting in an old iron bathtub that he'd set out on the deck. She was naked, soap suds just about covering her. Marty was standing behind Ray.

'Fookin' hell,' said Sylvio.

'Yeah,' said Marty. 'That's it, man. That's the one.'

8. The Hacienda

'I have a surprise,' said Iris.

I was lying on her bed. She was dressing.

'Good or bad?'

She turned to me for a moment. 'Good, silly. Do you want to come to the hacienda?'

'Okay . . . What is it?'

'It's a hacienda,' she said slowly. 'You know what one of those is, don't you?'

'I think so . . .'

'Okay . . . Well, we can fly down there today.'

'Fly? Where is it?'

Iris stared at me in the mirror she was using to put up her hair. 'It's a hacienda . . . It's in Cabo.'

'Cabo?'

'Yes, Cabo . . . *Jesus* . . . You know where Cabo is, right?'

I didn't, but I nodded anyway.

'It's my father's. We've been going ever since I can remember. Since I was little. It's cool there. You'll like it. We can swim and fuck.'

'I don't like swimming.' I paused. 'And if your father's going . . .'

'He's not, idiot,' she said. 'And I'll make you swim. There are two spaces on the plane. Get dressed.'

With that she went downstairs. When I got there, Brenna was in her office outfit again, making breakfast. Her ass strained against the skirt. The gods were either for me or against, I didn't know which. I began to wonder if this was what madness felt like.

'Iris, I may have to take some work with me,' I said. 'There's Matthew . . . this story . . . do you have a phone there?'

She gave me another look, the same one as I saw in the mirror upstairs. 'Of course it has a phone,' she said. 'That's fine. We'll come back on Sunday anyhow.'

I realised I had no idea what day it was. The concept of time was another that was eluding me.

'You been to Mexico before?' Brenna asked.

So that's where it was.

'No.' I thought for a second. 'Will I be able to get in? I don't have a visa . . .'

Brenna smirked. 'You won't need one,' she said.

Iris nodded. 'Uh huh.'

'Why wouldn't I need a visa?'

'It's a private airfield. You just give the guys there a few dollars and they'll let you through. The only passports they'll check on the way back are Mexican ones – not that there are any . . .'

'They know my father too. Don't worry. We've taken lots of people there.'

'You sure you can't come?' Iris said to Brenna.

Brenna stared at me hard. 'Don't be silly,' she said.

We drove out to the little airport in Burbank. The plane was the smallest I'd ever been on. There were maybe ten or twelve of us, and we filled it up. Most of the other passengers seemed to know Iris. The pilot greeted her with a kiss on both cheeks. He led us out across the tarmac. When we were all inside, he pulled a small screen across to divide us from the cockpit. The seats were leather, worn but soft. The stewardess operated a tiny galley at the back. From it she produced wines, spirits, cocktails, cheese, bread and cold meats. Everyone chatted happily as she brought what they wanted.

The pilot came on the intercom. ' We're set, folks,' he said. 'You all buckle up now.'

The plane charged down the runway and lurched into the air. The air pulsed against it. We heard the rudders creak as the pilot operated them. As we banked, one wing rose high above the other and it felt as though we would be tilted out of our seats. My stomach lurched and I squeezed Iris's hand. Iris and the others seemed completely unconcerned. We ploughed into the upper air. At a certain angle, the wind sang across the wings. After a while the keen pitch of the engines evened out and we flew more smoothly, the nose of the little plane slightly higher than the tail. The pilot slid his screen back. I could see out of his cockpit window into the endless blue in front of us. For some reason, it settled me down. I sucked on my beer and stared downwards through the window at my side. Underneath us were arid brown plains, vast and empty, that stretched to the jagged coast. We flew above the land's edge for most of the way, the crystalline sea contrasted against it. After a couple of hours, the nose of the plane dipped and the engine note lowered and we began to slip downwards, the air pressure heavy in my ears. Iris had worked her way through a couple of tall gins. She smiled happily. She placed her mouth to my ear.

'I can't wait for you to see the place,' she said. 'You'll like it.' She slid a hand on to my leg. 'I've been thinking about us being there . . .'

We hit a pocket of air and dropped lower, my stomach lurching upwards in response. I felt pale, clammy. I thought about how easy it would be to scream. The pilot slid his screen back again.

'Just a patch of cooler air, folks. We'll be on the ground soon . . .'

'Not that soon, I hope,' I said to Iris, but she wasn't listening to the pilot or me, instead she dreamily finished her drink.

The roofs of the houses that lined the coast became distinct. We flew over a little cluster of peasant casas and then, as we slowed, we floated above walled estates with lush, irrigated gardens that contrasted with the brown dirt of the surrounding roads and pathways. We made our approach from over the sea, swinging out beyond the coast-line, the white caps of the waves apparently close enough to touch. The wheels hit hard. A couple of glasses clinked. The plane taxied for a while and then came to a halt. I leaned back in the seat, feeling far better. Brenna was right about the terminal. Iris handed a few dollars to a kid in an overlarge hat who sat at a tiny desk and he scrawled something in my passport without even looking up.

Iris told the cab driver, in apparently perfect Spanish, to take us to the hacienda via the coast road – 'It's the long way around but I want you to see it,' she said – and as we rode, she told me about the fishing villages of San Lucas and San José that had still been a few miles apart when Iris was a kid but were now slowly becoming one, the Balnearios joining them together. She showed me El Arco, the great arc of rock on the edge of the peninsula, and the little restaurants on the seafront where she'd first eaten octopus and sea snails. We drove past long white playas where Iris had for the early years of her childhood been the only American kid (yet within two years of our visit, Cabo would be fully trans-formed into the rock-star destination of choice; Van Halen's singer Sammy Hagar had bought a place and would write a song called 'Cabo Wabo' for the band's next album. He also started a chic tequila business that he would later sell for tens of millions of dollars).

The hacienda stood at the end of a long dirt track outside of San José town, the cab bumping over its ruts and potholes, its engine note tight and high. We went through a set of gateposts with worn stone stallion heads on them bleached and dried. The paddocks on either side of the track were dry scrub, the stable buildings chained shut, but beyond them, on the approach to the house, was a green and shaded palm garden and two courtyards, a hammock strung between two palms in one, wrought-iron table and chairs under the giant tournefortia in the other, and a dense vine clinging to a trellis on the house itself.

Iris took a key from one of her bags and got the door open. Inside the air was warm and stale. The cab driver dropped the rest of the bags in the hall. Iris spoke to him in Spanish and handed him some notes.

'*Bueno, bueno, mañana,*' he said.

Iris led me through the stone-floored hallway and past a double staircase that led up to a circular mezzanine, and into a huge lounge room with a verandah beyond. She began opening blinds and lifting shutters and the late afternoon light flooded in. We went upstairs. Iris indicated an arched wooden double door.

'My father's room' she said. 'We won't go in there.'

Instead we went to Iris's, which was grand enough, with a little sitting room, a walk-in wardrobe, a sleek bathroom of steel and glass and then her bed itself, raised on a dais and with a view out over the walled garden. I understood now why Iris had laughed when I'd asked her if they had a telephone here.

The night seemed to come out of nowhere in Cabo; it was

sunlight and then the great black canopy with nothing in between. Iris lit candles on the verandah. The cicadas sang. She brought wine and pasta from the kitchen. After a while the wind got up and the candles started to flicker madly so we went inside.

★

The next morning the cab driver was back. He took us to the playa. It was almost deserted, just a few people sitting on the rocks where the beach began to curve from view. Iris spread a towel on the sand. She pulled off her T-shirt and skirt and lay in her white bikini, the light like a blade on her shins. I sat there in my clothes. Beaches weren't my thing, but I didn't have the heart to tell Iris. I watched the sea. After a while, a container ship appeared on the horizon. It slowly grew closer. It must have been a quarter of a mile long. On its deck stood piles of iron crates. I thought of Doc, his boats full of dope on a coastline somewhere across the vast Gulf of Mexico. Even the container was dwarfed by the seas it sailed through, a tiny speck of nothing. You could do anything you wanted out there. I thought of Iris's father too, his house in the hills, the place on Fountain, the estate on the coast, the hacienda and who knew what else.

'Did you have a globe when you were a kid?' I asked Iris. She was lying back on her towel, her sunglasses pushed up into her hair.

'Hmmm?' she said.

'It's only when you look at a globe that you understand how big the oceans are.'

'Hmmm,' she said again.

'What did you say your father did?'

'Oh cars, you know. Property now.'

'Did you ever wonder how he made so much money?'

'I don't think he does . . .'

'Really?'

'Blair's father is way richer. All of the girls I went to school with . . .' She pushed herself up on to her elbows and pulled down her sunglasses. We looked out at the sea. 'It hurt me when he stopped loving this place,' Iris said.

'Why did that happen?'

'My mother, I think. They used to come here when they were first together. He found the hacienda for her. She loved horses . . . The stables were her favourite place. She'd ride all day while my father was working. I'd come to the playa with the other kids.'

The container appeared to have moved a few inches along the horizon.

'What happened?'

'She went, I guess . . . My father and I were down here for a day or so. She was due to join us and she never came. I was still small but I remember my dad driving us to the airport, and watching for her to come off the plane, and she wasn't there. My father must have suspected it was going to happen. He must have told me something, explained why she wasn't there, but I don't think I was unhappy about it.'

'When did you realise she wasn't coming back?'

I waited for an answer but Iris seemed to be retreating from the memory.

'It wasn't so weird . . . I don't know if I thought about it very much. But afterwards I kind of knew that we only came back here because I loved it.'

She lay back down. We were silent for a while. The sun

beat down on the playa. Iris took my hand. 'You don't like the beach much, do you?' she said.

⋆

I had to write. The next morning, the cab driver was back at the hacienda. Iris told me that she was going shopping in Cabo and would be gone all day.

'When I get back, I've got a surprise for you . . .' she said, and slunk out.

I called Donald and spoke to Matthew. I had a long conversation with Geoff back at the magazine in London (keeping my exact whereabouts deliberately vague . . .). He'd got the copies of Donald's evidence that I'd mailed him and was ready to run the story. I sat at the old walnut desk that overlooked the verandah. Iris had found a typewriter somewhere. I set it up. I rolled in the paper and played about with intros, trying to get something that fitted the scale of the story. I was trying for something symbolic, maybe mythic (my memories of exactly what are indistinct now but I recall, with a shudder, something about circuses and masks and ringmasters . . . Frank Zappa once described the music press as 'people who can't write interviewing people who can't talk for people who can't read', a statement that shivers with truth). I felt the usual self-loathing as I stared out over the gardens. Finally I got a simple line: 'Who is Nikki Sixx?' and I was away. Something flowed. I wrote for a few hours, only occasionally stopping to check my notes, instead just getting the story down as Matthew had told it to me. The rest could wait. I went to the fridge and got a beer. I sat at the desk and read over what I'd written. I had the voice in my head, felt the rhythms of Matthew's speech on the page, the sad little sing-song of his stutter. The beer buzz settled. I began to write more. I felt like I was breaking through into somewhere, a sunlit upland. What a writer I was! I got more beer, carried on, the typewriter rocking on the creaking desk. Soon I was gazing out over the gardens in a mid-afternoon haze. Two beers – I wasn't exactly Hemingway, in either respect. I stacked the pile of paper by the typewriter. I drifted around the house for a while, enjoying the sensation of being alone there. It felt furtive, illicit. I found myself on the mezzanine outside Iris's father's room.

I held the door handles for a second and then pushed them inwards expecting to find them locked, but instead they swung open silently on their smooth hinges. I saw an old stone doorstop just inside and pinned one door back so that I would hear Iris if she returned unexpectedly. I was in a dark hallway. A face flashed in front of me and my stomach turned over, but on second glance it was an ornate Día de Muertos mask, its forehead and jawbone painted with jagged red and yellow lines, its eye sockets black and empty. At the end of the hallway was a study, and off that, the main bedroom, larger than Iris's. In the afternoon stillness it felt unlived in, the decor older than the rest of the house. It was real 1970s stuff, panelled wood, concealed lighting, a shag rug, one wall painted an acid orange, and in the centre a vast round bed sunk into the floor. The en suite was shabby too, a few old bottles of cologne on a glass shelf the only real sign of her father's presence. I pulled back a curtain. The view was out over the paddocks – he could have lain in bed in the early mornings watching his wife ride. There were silver-framed pictures on the dresser – a baby I presumed was Iris, kids in the sand on the playa, Iris's blonde hair picking her out among the locals, a couple of Iris's father, tanned and smiling, the images bleached by the sun. There was another that I thought was of Iris, a tall and slender figure in a sundress, framed in a doorway that I recognised as the kitchen downstairs, but when I picked it up and looked more closely I wasn't so sure. The picture had faded and behind the girl was an old stove that wasn't there any more. I replaced the picture carefully back against the thin line of dust that had gathered at its base.

I poked around in the study – a pair of boxing gloves hanging from a nail in the wall, old magazines stacked on the desk, mostly about cars, a couple of copies of *Rolling Stone*, a fountain pen and, up on a little shelf, three bullets, small grey slugs, obviously spent. I slid open a drawer. The first thing I saw was the gun, unholstered and lying on some papers. I picked it up. It was heavy and cold. I knew nothing about guns but even I could see it was a serious weapon, a semi-automatic, the clip sticking out from the bottom of the handle. I wasn't too alarmed. Almost everyone in LA had one somewhere. Sylvio had shown me Marty's little armoire: it bristled with pistols and rifles. I guessed you'd want a gun around if you were the rich gringos in 1970s Cabo, too. As I replaced the gun I noticed a pack of Polaroid images that had been underneath it. I set the gun on the desktop and pulled them out. They were of Iris's father and Brenna. In the first they were standing together, her head on his shoulder; the rest they seem to have taken of one another, Iris's father shirtless, Brenna topless, and then naked on the bed that was just behind me. I pushed them back into the packet and put the gun on top of them, shutting the drawer and quickly leaving the room. I slid the doorstop away and closed the doors, wishing now I'd never gone in.

★

I was reading when Iris got back. The disaffected LA rich kids of the book had heard about the rumoured existence of a snuff movie, a notion that didn't seem entirely impossible in the city's haunted canyons – something that gnawed at my sense of unease (which in turn was compounded by being alone in an isolated house, a gun in a drawer upstairs – I realised that afternoon that aside from Brenna and Iris, absolutely no one in the world knew that I was here), so I was glad to hear the cab pull up and Iris clatter on to the flagstones in her heels.

'Look what I've got for you,' she said, her eyes glittering. In her hands were a couple of tickets. I went to take them from her but she drew back.

'A kiss first,' she said. It felt good to hold her, to have human contact. She sat in my lap and showed me the tickets. They were for a night of boxing at the town hall in St Lucas.

'I saw it when we came in,' she said, 'and I knew we had to go. It'll be fun. They love the fighting down here. I used to go with my father whenever it was on.'

I recalled Iris's father's early years as a boxer. We'd had a semi-drunken conversation about it the night we spent at the beach house, Sherry's eyes glazing over with boredom as Iris laughed and spoke about the boxers she liked. Her favourite was Julio Cesar Chavez, the indomitable Mexican champion who'd grown up in an abandoned railway car. I liked him too. He tried to knock out everyone they put in front of him. I liked the guys who fought like they were stood on the lip of the grave: Benn, Hearns, Hagler, Sylvio's hero Durán. I liked them even more when they lost and then came back, damaged somehow; broken and even more magnificent for it. I liked the unlucky ones, the doomed, like Liston and Tyson and Kid Chocolate.

Iris showered and changed. She had her hair up and wore a cocktail dress and heels.

'They dress for the fights here,' she said.

I went upstairs. I found a half-decent shirt and put it on. Iris arrived to look me over. She tutted and left. I heard her cross the mezzanine. The handles on the doors to her father's room clicked. I hoped I'd put everything I'd touched back properly but I couldn't be sure. She was in there a while. She came back with a sports jacket over one arm and a bottle of the cologne I'd seen in the bathroom.

'Don't be so nervous,' she said, 'it'll look good . . .'

I put the jacket on. It fitted okay, even though Iris's father had seemed much bigger than me. She pulled at the lapels.

'Not bad . . .' she said, and then sprayed some of the cologne on to my neck and the shoulders of the jacket. 'Hmmm,' she went on. 'I like that smell . . .'

The cab driver seemed delighted to see Iris again, despite his many trips to the hacienda. He drove us along darkened lanes, the car bouncing on the rutted surface, and then on to the little highway into town. He and Iris spoke in Spanish. I heard the words 'El Diablo' and they both laughed.

The traffic grew heavier and by the time we reached the main square we were travelling at the same speed as the people who were walking languidly along the middle of the road. We jumped out, Iris handing over more dollars, and joined the queue at the entrance to the town hall.

Inside was an echoing room with a domed ceiling, a temporary boxing ring at its centre and a large lighting galley hanging over it, suspended from the beams by thick cable. There were a few roped-off rows of seats around the ring. Beyond them, everyone stood. A group of kids were selling beer in paper cups. I bought a couple, and Iris squeezed her way through to the seats and handed over our tickets. She was right, inside the ropes were girls in evening wear and guys in suits.

Iris and I watched the whole thing, starting with the first prelim. She sat hunched forwards on her seat, hands in her lap, dress riding up, clicking her heels on the floor. She watched each fight intently. In between we talked and she drank her beer from the paper cup. The main event ended early, a second-round KO from a squat Mexican brawler, the crowd shouting 'El Diablo . . . El Diablo' as he worked his man over on the ropes, digging him hard in the ribs, following through with his elbows, rubbing the top of his head into the other guy's puffy, reddening face . . .

Iris wasn't finished. We stayed for the floating bouts. The last of them was a six-rounder at lightweight. One skinny white boy was in the red corner. Another skinny white boy was in the blue. I loved this moment, when they stood before the bell, with the seconds sent out and the referee looking at the timekeeper. They were perfectly alone. Their torsos twitched and flickered. They were bare and raw, luminous almost. They stepped forward towards one another with nothing but their thin bodies to help them. Only they knew if they had prepared well enough, and sometimes even they didn't know. You could see it.

The two boys went at each other. Iris and I could hear everything; their feet squeaking on the canvas as they dug for purchase, their grunts and squeals, the snot fired out of their noses. The bright lights showed up the acne on their backs, the rope marks and the blood puffing out their faces as they swelled and marked with the punches they received.

In between each round, the blue corner's trainer would scream at his man in disgust:

'Can't you move? Can't you duck? Can't you throw a left? Do you want this or are you wasting my time?'

The kid would slump on his stool. When the ten-second warning sounded, the trainer would grab his man by both cheeks and say 'I love you' and then throw him towards the centre of the ring.

By the sixth, blue corner was sagging. He took two horrid shots on the ear and went down. When he stood up again, he almost heaved. His eardrum had gone. He was sick and unbalanced. His trainer wrapped him up in a white towel and screamed at him: 'I love you, man . . . I love you.'

As the loser stepped down from the ring, I looked around and saw that most of the crowd had left. The kid walked past us, deathly pale. As he did Iris put out her hand and gently stroked his shoulder. I put my arm round Iris in the same way and walked her out on to the square. We didn't speak. We were feeling the sadness of the fight.

She led us to a little bar on the far side of the square where inside it was dark and cool and we drank a couple more beers. I took Iris's hand. 'Thanks,' I said. 'That was good wasn't it . . . hard but good . . .'

'It was. I hope that boy is alright.'

'He may not fight again.'

'I hope he doesn't. He wasn't that great . . .'

'How come they have American fighters down here?'

'We like to see the gringos beat each other up . . .'

'We?'

Iris laughed. '*Si. Viva el Mexicanos* . . .'

'Did you father ever fight here?' I thought of the boxing gloves hanging in his study.

'I don't think so,' she said. 'We didn't come to Cabo until he had some money, so he'd finished by then.'

'Do you think he was good?'

'El Diablo,' she smiled. 'He'd be like that. He's one of those people who never gives up . . .' She drained her beer.

'Chugalug,' I said.

'Chugalug . . . You know that thing I told you about that happened to me, when I was fifteen, at Blair's house . . . Brenna was going to bring me down here to sort it out. It was the first thing that we thought of, but I'm glad we didn't . . . Come on, let's go . . .'

We found the cab driver in the taxi rank and he began his latest trip out to the hacienda. He and Iris gabbled away about El Diablo for a while. It seemed to re-energise her. The cab jolted along the track to the house. Iris bounced through the door, throwing on lights.

'Get towels,' she said. I had no idea why, but we picked some up and she led me outside to the walled garden and through a little gate at the back, almost hidden by the tournefortia. Behind it was a courtyard I hadn't seen before with a small swimming pool. Iris threw switches and the courtyard lit up. The pool had lights buried in the bottom too, and marble edges all around it.

'Look,' said Iris pointing at it. 'Cool, huh . . .'

On the bottom of the pool was another Día de Muertos skull, picked out in mosaic tiles. It stared up at us through the water.

'I call him Charlie,' she said. 'He gets a good view of everything that goes on here . . .'

She smirked and pulled her dress over her head. I had a good view too. She slipped into the pool and swam a couple of lengths in her easy, athletic way. Her body shimmered beneath the skin of the water.

'Come on,' she said. 'Get in . . .'

I pulled off my clothes. I was the whitest man in Cabo,

maybe on the whole continent. Even Iris looked tan in comparison. I shivered a little, although the air was still and warm. Swimming, the beach . . . it was a different world to me. I edged into the water. It was okay, not too bad. I swam an exploratory length of the pool. I made it. I waited a minute and then came back. Iris swam over.

'How did I end up with someone like you?' she said.

★

Later, we lay upstairs and I read Iris what I'd written about Matthew Trippe and Nikki Sixx. She stared up at the ceiling while she listened. The big clock in the hallway ticked. As I read, images came into my head, images of the dark seas of Carolina and the dark house beneath us. When we woke the next morning, Iris told me about the dream she'd had, of Donald setting up a series of meetings with her at Doc McGhee's offices, and at each one telling her that Matthew and Nikki and Frankie Feranna were all the same person, but she and he were the only ones who knew.

She took one last trip into Cabo while I went through the story and rewrote the parts I didn't like. Iris had been gone about an hour when the telephone rang. For no logical reason, it spooked me. I let it ring a little longer while I ran through the possibilities of who it could be. It rang on. Most likely it was Iris calling from town, wanting me to pick up. I did. I said nothing, waiting for a voice on the other end, but none came, instead just the distance and the echo of an open line, long distance, far away, and then the click of disconnection. I went back to the desk but got nothing done. Fifteen minutes later (I was watching the clock) it rang again, for a long time. I knew what would happen. Another fifteen minutes and it began to ring. I got a grip, realised my cowardice. I grabbed the receiver.

'Hello?'

I heard, or rather felt, the presence on the end of the line; it was as though someone was standing behind me, unseen. After ten seconds or so whoever it was exhaled (male, it sounded male), and just before the line went dead, there was the sound of movement in the background, a door closing with a hard click. I shivered. The hands on the clock moved towards the next quarter-hour, but passed by without another call.

Iris got back soon afterwards. I followed her like a whipped dog as she threw the clothes she'd left strewn over the bed into her case. I gathered my things, too. The cab was outside. We walked through the little airport at Cabo without a word from the kid at the desk – still the same guy – and went out to the plane across the parched concrete. It swung out over the ocean in a wide turn, and I leaned over Iris to see El Arco for the last time. The rudders in the wings clicked and soon the rocks were just a single line of definition against the water. Iris fell asleep and didn't stir until we arrowed down towards Burbank. The wheels bounced crazily on the runway and one wing dipped towards the ground, but we were okay.

It was only later that I realised that this was the moment that one thing had become another.

*

It was late afternoon when we got back to the house on Fountain. We dumped the bags and drove to the Hyatt so that I could use the fax machine to get the Matthew story to Geoff for Monday morning in England. While I did, Iris rang up to Ray's room, and discovered him at the roof bar with Marty and Sylvio. They were deep in discussion. Things had been happening in the few days we'd been away. Lana had been offered a tour, third on a three-band bill opening up for a gruesome shock metal band with delusions of grandeur (they'd just made a concept album that they were comparing to *Tommy*) and a German techno-thrash band with an unintelligible concept record of their own. The shows were 2,000- and 3,000-seaters, a swing through Texas and the South as far as Florida. The buy-on was $20,000 with a guarantee of a half-hour set plus soundcheck, and a corner of the merchandise stall. Marty had to decide whether to pay it or not.

Ray and I had worked with the shock metal band before. Their singer was an ageing and bombastic dick convinced of his own genius called Steevi Blue. I disliked him intensely. A few months before, we'd spent an unpleasant evening in the Rainbow, him bored and distracted, looking up from his drink to point at the girls circling the little horseshoe of VIP seats.

'Fucked her,' he said, gesturing openly at one. 'Fucked her, too . . . and her. I fucked her. Her too. And that one there.'

One of the girls began to glare at him aggressively. He didn't seem to notice.

'What's the problem with her?' I asked him.

'I dunno, I probably screwed her too and don't remember it. Or screwed her friend instead. Hey, honey . . .' He gave her a sarcastic wave. She glared back some more. I went to the restroom wondering how he did it. Blue had a balloon head and scarecrow hair, and up close his age was beginning to tell. His face was puffy and his skin blotched. When I got back, the girl who had been glaring at him was sitting on his lap. He still looked bored and distracted. Then his manager arrived, Rex, a sharp English guy with a Cambridge degree, and drove us out to an all-night video shoot for the next single, high up in the hills, where the lights and the noise had attracted a local loon who'd begun firing a rifle at us. We'd spent a couple of hours cowering in the production truck while the cops tried to find him. When they did, it turned out to be an air gun ('That's bullshit, man,' Blue had said after they'd gone – he'd spent most of the two hours in the truck droning on about all of the obsessed fans and jealous boyfriends who'd wanted to kill him). Even Ray was ambivalent towards Blue, and I found it hard to think of anyone he felt that way about.

We'd worked with the German thrash band as well. They were managed by Rex too. They seemed to spend most of their time on tour taking photographs of everything. Their attitude to heavy metal was interesting and fitted with most German acts: they loved the slapstick element of it, they gurned their way through gigs, but they took the music itself deeply seriously. What was missing was irony and self-awareness.

I joined Iris just as Marty disappeared for a piss. The atmosphere was strangely tense.

'Fookin' idiot,' Sylvio said. 'What's fookin' twenty grand to him? He's got an album on the cheap, now he wants a free tour? Fookin' not going to happen, mate . . .'

Marty got back just as Ray was explaining that he'd already arranged for me and him to travel to some of the dates. The magazine would take a feature on Blue, a full-page review of the show, and would extend the piece we were doing on Lana even further if she ended up playing too.

'It does sound good,' Iris said. She seemed to be the only one of us whom Marty really took any notice of.

'What about the crowds?' he asked.

'They're a nice fit,' Iris said. 'They'll be ninety-nine per cent boys, young . . . The last time Blue played in LA, he had a naked woman strapped to a rack on stage . . .'

Marty's expression hardened at that.

'She's right.' I stepped in. 'It's the same crowd Lana would get in England. Blue's full of shit, but it'll sell out. Can you get the record in the stores in time?'

'It ships next week,' he said. He seemed to be coming around a little. 'You're not rehearsed,' he said to Sylvio.

'It's a half-hour set. We just spent three weeks playing the fookin' thing in the studio. It's not exactly Abraxas, is it?'

'What do you think it will cost all in?' Marty asked Iris.

'If you load in yourselves and use their desk and sound crew so that it's just the band in the bus, share rooms in the hotels, it'll be about a thousand a week. If you do okay on the merch you can pull some of that back . . . How many shows are you getting?'

'Twenty.'

'If you can get local press and radio, it's not a bad deal . . . I can probably help you a little with that.'

Marty turned to Sylvio.

'What do we pay Tony and Doug?'

'Two hundred a week. Plus all accommodation and meals.'

'Can't they sleep on the bus?'

'If you get a big enough bus . . .'

'That would probably cost you more than the hotels,' Iris said. She was used to all of this – almost every band on her label would be running on the same economics. 'And you have to pay secure parking each night. It's not worth it.'

'What's the alternative?' I asked Marty. 'Wait around here for a few club shows? It'll look good back in England too.'

'And we definitely get a bigger piece in the magazine?' he asked Ray.

'Yes, darling.'

Marty looked out over the rail at the traffic on Sunset. 'Okay,' he said evenly. 'I'll make the call.'

'Where's Lana?' I asked.

'She's got a singing lesson,' Ray replied. I laughed, but choked it back when I saw the look on Marty's face. He stomped off to use the phone.

Later Rex, Steevi Blue's manager, showed up. He told us he'd driven down from his new house in the hills. He said that he was renting it from David Lee Roth. 'You guys should come up sometime,' he said. 'Bit different from England. This is the fucking life, I'll tell you boys.'

He signalled to the waiter with an easy authority that brought the guy running over.

'Now my friend,' he said. 'In approximately fifteen minutes' time, I want you to bring the biggest fucking bottle of bubbles you've got over to this table, okay?' He proffered him a couple of hundred-dollar bills. 'And you keep it coming. Fifteen minutes, son, okay?'

He turned away from the waiter and reached inside his jacket. From it he took a contract. 'Might as well get this sorted now,' he said to Marty, and handed it over. 'It's all as I told you on the phone.'

Marty took off his sunglasses and sat down to read. Fifteen minutes later he was done. He took out his pen and scrawled a signature two or three times across the pages.

'Quick way to spend your money, isn't it, lad?' Rex said.

Marty forced out a smile. 'My office will wire it over first thing.'

Right on cue, the waiter returned with the champagne.

'Looks like we're going on tour, boys,' Sylvio said, and started to drink.

★

The night had got messy. Iris and I woke up in the other bed in Ray's suite, Ray emerging from the shower with an arched eyebrow, my head full of wool, my mouth filled with ash. Rex had kept the champagne coming, his easy charm working its way through Marty like a good massage. He'd told us outrageous stories of his early days in management, the fast talking and the bullshit when he had everything on the line, the record companies he'd bluffed, the A&R guys he'd played off against one another. He used an old Don King trick to get his first band, a then-hot young London act who already had a manager and record companies swarming all over them. He'd rung the record company that they really wanted to sign with and asked if they would be interested in meeting with the band if he brought them in. They agreed. Then he went to see the band when he knew their manager wouldn't be around and told them he'd been authorised by the record label to set up a meeting. They agreed too. He'd inserted himself into the deal, and it began. He claimed he used his maths degree to reinvent the way a rock band made their money. He worked out that a T-shirt with the band's logo could be sold for the same price as a record, except the band got ten per cent of the revenue generated by record sales and one hundred per cent generated by T-shirts sold at gigs. He made sure the band had specially created artwork for every tour, and made them millionaires from T-shirt sales long before they were millionaires from record sales (though they had accomplished that too). He hadn't stopped there. He stood around at the merchandise stalls in concert halls and asked the kids how much money they had to spend. He calculated that the average was twenty bucks, and so he priced his T-shirts at ten, his tour books at five, his sweatbands at two, his button badges at a dollar, and so on. He took everything that they brought with them. He had solid steel cases made that could hold exactly $100,000 in cash and when their last US tour was over, he threw them all in the hold of their private plane and flew straight to Switzerland, where he banked it all without paying tax anywhere.

He'd sorted out one musician's divorce by handing over one of those cases to his former wife, a stripper he'd insisted on marrying after a three-day hotel-room party (another old Don King trick – street hustlers will always take a suitcase of money now over the promise of a cheque tomorrow, however big that cheque might actually be) and he'd bought each member of the band houses in Spain without telling them (they'd all sold them a couple of years later after they'd doubled in value).

By the time he'd finished talking, Marty was practically taking notes. He'd probably had $20,000-worth of free advice while he was drinking Rex's champagne.

By the time Rex was done, we were the last people left on the roof (he'd downed the final bottle while standing on a table, trying to point out his house among the lights twinkling in the distant hilltops). He walked away whistling, the back of his expensive jacket covered in a large patch of sweat. Sylvio had lit a cigar and was sitting back in his chair with his eyes closed, a look of unsurpassable happiness on his face. I turned and whispered to Iris, 'Can you believe we were at the hacienda this morning?' She slid her hand on to my leg and looked at me with bombed-out eyes. It felt like a day that had lasted for two.

I wondered if she would remember promising Marty that she'd come on the road too (in thrall to the power of Rex, he'd begun offering her increasing sums of money to look after the press and PR). I had another nagging recollection that I'd told Rex what I thought of Steevi Blue, but I couldn't be sure.

We'd hauled ourselves out of Ray's bed and downstairs into the smiting heat of the mezzanine car park. I drove Iris out to her office (she'd walked inside with a slight but noticeable stiffness to her gait, quiet and pale and sick) and then went back to the Hyatt to meet Ray. We went to the Denny's just down the Strip where I just about kept down some eggs and hash browns while Ray told me the real reason that Lana had not been at the Hyatt – Marty had raged at her after he'd discovered that she'd been alone in the house with Doug the day that Sylvio and I had called around unexpectedly. Doug's presence on the road was part of the reason Marty had been so reluctant to agree to the tour – it was starting too quickly to recruit anyone else. Now Doug was going and Marty was coming too.

'Do you think there's really anything between them?' I asked Ray.

'Dunno,' he said. 'There's definitely a vibe, but that doesn't mean that they're doing each other. If I had to guess, I'd say she's using Doug to wind her husband up a little, that's all. Marty's insecure, but so is Lana. I don't think she would have liked all of that talk about street hustlers that Rex gave us . . .'

He was probably right. Lana had none of Sylvio's apparently

indestructible confidence. I'd noticed a change in Sylvio too. Last night, when Marty had been refusing to cover the tour fee he'd become very angry, angrier than I'd ever seen him before. In the past he would have hidden it, thrown out a few bad jokes, come back with a different approach, a new angle to gain the position that he wanted. I wondered why such a change had come.

9. Tour

We began in Phoenix four days later. Ray and I travelled with the band in the RV that Marty had hired, him at the wheel, the world's richest tour-bus driver. Iris was to join us in Houston. Marty had her on the payroll in some way or another – he'd negotiated some of her time at her record company job. I'd left her at the house with Brenna, who was still being glacial and detached with me; leaving Iris alone with her had seemed like a surrender of any control I had, and during the long and boring bus trip to Phoenix – there was a subdued tension to the journey that I was putting down to pre-tour nerves – I tried to ride out my anxiety. I needed Sylvio or Ray to pull me out of it but Ray slept most of the way and Sylvio was uncharacteristically withdrawn, having long, sotto voce discussions with Tony about the set that they'd been hurriedly rehearsing. There was something else too: the last evening before we'd left had been filled with phone calls to the magazine, where Geoff was getting ready to run the Matthew Trippe story. Somehow Doc had got wind and was laying siege with all kinds of threats, from libel to a withdrawal of access to any of his acts. Geoff had taken this as I knew he would – confirmation that it was a story with heat on it, although what sort of heat neither of us could be sure. We knew that Doc would have a good idea of the content having seen Donald's lawsuit, but there were many ways it could be told and the legalities were only one. We'd agreed that it was a good time for me to be out of LA all the same. By chance, on the morning we'd left I'd had another of Donald's clandestine calls – at that point he was the last person I wanted to hear from, but he offered me the number of Michael Aquino, the former US Army lieutenant colonel who was now the leader of the Temple of Set, the occult church that had sheltered Matthew after he'd been caught up in the armed robbery and whom Matthew had spoken about for a long time that day at the Roosevelt. I promised Donald I'd speak to him. Maybe I'd wait until Iris arrived out here until I did.

Phoenix was hot with a dry wind. We found the venue, a basketball arena way out in the suburbs by a giant Walmart and a parched shopping mall. People moved slowly around it. We found the production office. The tour manager was a classic of the type, stocky, muscled, tattooed, ponytailed, bearded, imparting a deep weariness to any enquiry or problem. Marty waved his contract about but was quickly chopped down by a terse list of instructions that let him know how much of the backline he was getting, which percentage of lights, what time they'd be soundchecking and for how long. He was dismayed to discover that there would be no road crew at all, and told Doug that he'd have to use the German speed metal band's drumkit. Marty began to bluster but the tour manager's attention was already elsewhere. We trooped around the arena looking for Lana's dressing room, which we eventually found located by a couple of store cupboards.

'Fuck,' Marty said when we got inside to find a few plastic chairs inside an otherwise cold and unaired room. We threw down a few bags and went back to the bus to get the gear.

The stage was already fully rigged, the curtain dropped halfway along its length to obscure Steevi Blue's show – he had a couple of steel cages either side of the riser, some oil drums painted up to look old and rusted, fake barbed wire

strung about the monitors and the infamous torture rack ready
to be pushed out from the wings. The effect was supposed to
be of a post-apocalyptic landscape ruled by Steevi and his band
but up close it looked like what it was – cheap and badly made.
Beyond the curtain, crammed on to the remaining stage space,
was the German speed metal band's drumkit. It must have
had fifteen or sixteen drums, great trees of cymbals, hanging
cowbells, wind chimes . . . It arced around in a large horseshoe.
Doug got behind it and disappeared. Sylvio and Tony plugged
their amp heads into the cabinets and began to soundcheck.
Lana arrived halfway through. They played a little more and
then stopped.

'Alright love,' she said, peering out from the stage edge
towards the mixing desk. 'We can't really hear owt up here.'

The sound engineer twiddled with the monitor mix. They
started playing again. It sounded exactly the same out in
the hall, but Lana and Sylvio seemed happy enough with it. The
engineer stuck some masking tape by the settings and marked
something on them. Without anyone in the arena, the music
bounced off the walls, thin and empty. They came to a halt
again. Tony jumped down and began asking the engineer
questions, but just then the Germans arrived and he told Tony
that they had to get off the stage. Tony began to argue but a
couple of roadies were already unplugging the cabinet heads.
Tony and Sylvio stomped off to find Marty, to whinge about
what twenty grand had bought them.

Ray and I decided to take a cab back into the city. There
was no torpor that quite matched the early afternoon on tour.
Every soundcheck I'd ever been at was exactly the same, and
so was every support act. They always felt hard done by. They
all swore that when they 'made it' they wouldn't treat their
own support in the same way, but they always did. The cycle

was permanent, only the faces changed. On the way out, we got sight of Steevi Blue. He gave us a surly stare, his scarecrow hair crammed under a baseball cap, and then he recognised Ray. We shook hands. He told us how great the show was. We told him how much we were looking forward to it. Insincerity dripped from us all. He disappeared into the dark of the corridor.

'I need a beer,' said Ray, and walked quickly towards the cab rank that sat across the giant car parks by the never-closing mall.

★

The cab driver took us to a bar called the 58. It had five other people inside, two couples at the darkened tables, an old girl on her own on a stool by the bar. The waitresses were topless. Ours came over.

'Hi,' she said, in a sing-song voice. 'Welcome to the 58, my name's Nancy.'

'Hello Nancy,' said Ray.

'So have you guys ever been to the 58 before? Okay, well let's find you a table and we'll get you started on some drinks . . .'

Nancy seemed impossibly cheerful for a young and beautiful girl spending a hot afternoon in a maid's apron and heels serving drinks to men twice her age – well in Ray's case at least. I tried hard not to stare at her tits while she ran through the menu and the various charges. (The 58 seemed to be some kind of clip joint dressed with the slightest suggestion of something more sophisticated – it didn't matter to us. Ray had a pocket full of dollars that he been given by Rex, who knew how to keep the wheels greased.) She brought us some beers and a tall glass of sparkling water for herself. She sat down.

'So,' she said. 'What brings you boys to town?'

We told her. Nancy gave a little squeal. She was a reader of the magazine. She had tickets to the show. She was funny and sweet. I wished that she had some clothes on. 'Hey, buy some more beers and ask me for a shot of tequila,' she said. 'I can slip it in here.' She touched the bottom of her glass. Ray offered her a twenty. 'I'd like to drink it with you too,' she said. Ray pulled another twenty. Nancy slipped away to the bar. When she came back, she slid the drinks from the tray on to the table.

'Tell me when the woman at the bar isn't looking at us,' she said.

'She's the boss, then?'

'Yeah, and she's a bitch.'

Ray gave Nancy a nod, and she quickly tipped the tequila into her drink. She took a mouthful. 'That's better,' she said.

We sat in the artificial semi-dark. Nancy told us that working at the 58 was better than her last job, which was at the giant Walmart out by the arena. 'I'd never have met you guys at Walmart,' she said. 'So that's good. Old guys some-times try to grab my tits, so that's bad . . .' She laughed. 'My boyfriend doesn't like it, but hey . . . I want to go to LA anyhow. It sucks here.' Nancy's boyfriend was in a band. She thought that they could make it in LA too.

'They're really cool,' she said. 'Honestly, you guys should see them.' She drained her glass and leaned towards Ray, pushing her breasts together with her arms. 'Shall we have some more?' She went to the bar.

'We're exactly the sort of guys she preys on,' I said. 'An afternoon to kill, and someone else's money.'

'Hmmm,' he said. 'Good, isn't it . . .' He raised his beer and drained it. Nancy came back with more drinks. This time there were two shots of tequila on the tray. Ray gave her a nod and she slipped them into her water. She drank quite quickly this time, the alcohol animating her, underlining the blank and cheerful facade which she'd used to greet us. It was worse somehow. Now she had hope.

We stayed another hour in the 58. Nancy spoke about her dreams of LA. Ray talked to her gently, telling her how it would be, never disillusioning her. He was good at this: strange girls, new cities. He had genuine empathy. Before we left he took off his pass and gave it to Nancy. 'Oh my God,' she said, several times. She slipped it in the pocket of her apron and kept sliding her hand in to touch its edge. 'Oh my God,' she said again. 'Do you think I'll meet Steevi Blue? I really like him. What's he like?'

I thought of Steevi Blue in the Rainbow, in all of his corruption. I took another drink and told Nancy all about him.

*

Outside the 58, Phoenix was hot in the late afternoon, the sun still above the tall buildings of downtown, casting deep shadows into their canyons. We found a cab. I rolled down the window, grateful for the breeze. I felt soporific, the weight of the dead hours bearing down. The show was still another three away. This was, I was quickly remembering, the rhythm of touring, an alien physical and mental state that only seemed to become normalised after years of doing it. I wondered if we would ever see Nancy again. I wondered if she should move to LA, live the cliché, have her dream, become a waitress or a hostess, living through some dark and messy years as the dream fades away, leave the city and go home before she got old (the thought of staying there afterwards seemed somehow worse, more desperate – the old really did disappear there . . .). Then I wondered about her not going, staying in Phoenix instead, her life drifting towards a suburban conclusion, having kids with a husband who was once in a band, a gentle regret at what might have been growing as the school runs piled on top of one another and the years passed by . . .

I came to with a start, Ray yanking on my arm. I'd fallen into a half-drunken sleep and drooled on my hand. I felt a dry line of pain emerging just above my eyelids.

'You were muttering in your sleep,' Ray said.

'I was thinking about Nancy . . .'

'I don't blame you, darling,' he said. 'Tremendous tits . . .'

We wandered around the corridors of the arena until we found the hospitality. Tony and Doug and a few members of the German speed metal band were already there, picking through the cooling pizza and buckets of fried chicken. They already had their stage gear on. It was typical German band stuff, tight leather S&M gear set off by bullet belts and cowboy boots.

'You can only get away with that in a metal band or a sex dungeon,' Tony said. Doug heard us and came over. I thought he'd been talking to one of the Germans – tall, long-haired, lots of flesh and straps and handcuffs – but when they turned around it was a girl, broad-shouldered and hard-bodied and wearing, along with the straps and the cuffs, a studded leather bikini.

'This is Nina,' he said. 'She's Steevi's rack girl . . .'

'Hey,' she said. We shook hands. Her grip was more powerful than mine. We air-kissed. She had a leather collar around her neck with long spikes sticking out of it. Nina was fun. She was another of Steevi's fans. 'That dick,' she said. 'Every night, I say to him, don't fuckin' rub so hard against me when I'm strapped up to that thing. I mean, I can feel his cock, man, and I don't want to feel his needle dick on me but every night, he rubs up harder . . .'

Marty appeared briefly, and ordered Tony and Doug back to the dressing room. I didn't see them again until they came out on stage. The arena was about half full. I watched from the side of the stage as people milled around. The house lights went down. Marty walked out to the microphone.

'Good evening Phoenix!' he shouted. 'Will you welcome, from London England . . .' He yelled Lana's name and ran off again. Doug jumped behind the giant drum kit. Sylvio walked on from the far wing and raised one arm above his head. Tony counted them in and they began. Lana came on and did her familiar little dance. I looked out into the hall. A few hundred people watched. Lana urged them on between songs and got a small cheer when she removed her jacket. I saw Tony raise an eyebrow towards Doug. Marty was writing in his notebook. Sylvio kept gesturing to the mixing desk. The sound clattered around the hall. The last song finished and they trooped off to some thin applause that quickly died. We sat in the dressing room in silence. Marty walked in and opened his notebook.

'Not now,' said Lana coldly. Marty closed the book and walked out again.

The Germans rattled past the door on their way to the stage. We heard the crowd roar as the lights went down.

'Cunts,' said Sylvio.

★

Ray and I stayed to see Steevi Blue. Doug stuck around too, but the others headed for the hotel. The arena had filled, and was now in darkness. Dry ice began pumping from the wings and, behind it, blinding floor lights turned the smoky clouds transluscent and silver. A portentous intro tape played. Steevi Blue appeared in silhouette, in Jesus Christ pose. The noise of the crowd rose, people whistled and yelled. Steevi Blue leaned back and let out a scream. The band kicked in. I had to admit, it was a moment. The lighting rig dropped down, illuminating the post-apocalyptic stage set. Steevi scuttled about it on pipe-cleaner legs, his shirt slashed to the waist. His massive head bobbed around. Next to him was Hulme, his lead guitar player. They had a famously fractious relationship. Hulme was giant blond Californian, a Valley guy with the physique of a heavyweight boxer who hadn't fought for a couple of years, a legendary drinker whose huge hands seemed to swallow most of the guitar he was holding. He wrangled riffs from it, twisting his left hand along the neck. Unlike Steevi, he spent most of his time at the edge of the stage, looking into the dark for women. When he saw one he liked, he'd stand and play right in front of her, his legs apart. The air had a chemical reek, the dry ice mixed with spilled beer and freshly lit dope. The crowd surged towards the points at which he stood. Between songs, Hulme took long swigs from a bottle of vodka. Sometimes he'd hand the bottle to one of the fans at the front of the stage so that they could drink too.

They had started with several of Steevi's old songs. They were about naked women and motorbikes and the kind of things that Steevi Blue did on both. They were dumb yet they had a kind of vicious desperation to them that spoke to a crowd like this one. But then they started playing Steevi's new concept album, its ten linked songs about an army of kids zombified by a religious television channel and now wandering across America in search of a messiah who kept appearing to them in a series of visions at cinemas and shopping malls and on jumbotrons outside of sports arenas. The crowd stayed with it for a while but they weren't really here for allegorical stories about the wasting of a generation. Hulme didn't seem to like it much either. During lengthening sections of Steevi's spoken-word narrations he left the stage and stood in the wings drinking more vodka. Steevi pressed on. This was his emergence as a serious artist. Eventually it ended, and the rack was pushed out on to the stage, this time with Nina dressed in her bondage gear and strapped to it. Steevi played his most famous song, 'I, Animal', and while Hulme took his solo he went over to the rack and rubbed himself up against Nina as she writhed. He brought out a whip and cracked it across her legs and arms. He grabbed her leather bra, pulled it down and smeared fake blood over her breasts. He rubbed his head between them and turned back to the crowd, his face smeared with the blood too. He stood at the front of the stage in his Christ pose, arms outstretched. The crowd swelled in front of him. I watched Nina climb off the rack in the semi-dark at the rear of the stage. She pulled up the leather bra and covered herself in a towel handed to her by one of the road crew. She disappeared towards the dressing rooms, gone before Steevi had finished thanking the crowd.

*

That night, or maybe it was the next in Corpus Christi (those first dates in Arizona and Texas, which ran into San Antonio and then down to the gulf at Houston, were a road trip of their own, the shining cars that passed us on the brown highways, the cities of silver and concrete looming up from the vast desert plains, the identical basketball arenas that hosted the shows, have all converged in the memory into one long, repeating day), Steevi and Hulme had a fight that threatened to throw the tour off the rails. We heard about it from Nina, who had taken to travelling on our bus for some of the journeys between shows, partly to spend as little time with Steevi as possible and partly because Ray had begun shooting some pictures of her in the bespoke 'performance art' bondage gear that she made.

The fight had begun when Steevi handed Rex a note and instructed him to give it to Hulme. The note ordered Hulme to stop going on stage without a shirt because it 'was putting off the chicks'. Hulme had sent one back that read, 'In that case, you should wear a brown bag over your head.' When Steevi read it, they'd squared up, Hulme laughing in Steevi's face. Hulme had walked on stage without his shirt and they'd played a violently loud set that was by a distance the best thing I'd heard them do. Afterwards Steevi brooded in his dressing room and Hulme got catastrophically drunk – he lay on a table in the catering room and poured two bottles of vodka into his mouth, something that reduced him to helpless laughter, and then to a sleep from which he was unrousable for some hours. Having been told by Rex that it would be too expensive to fire Hulme until the tour was complete, Steevi – a sullen drunk himself – had begun muttering darkly about calling on biker gangs who 'owed him big time' and then how often 'drunk drivers' like Hulme got in 'freeway wrecks'. . . A day later a 'personal trainer' had joined the tour and Steevi took daily workouts on the punchbag and the pads, his spider limbs flailing as his great face reddened (one afternoon, with Steevi absent, Hulme had thrown a careless left hand into the bag as he walked past, a blow that made it bounce on its chain – 'Now that guy can punch,' the trainer said to no one in particular, 'I'd like to train that guy . . .'). The tension hung over the subsequent days, with only the Germans apparently inured to it (they delivered the same relentlessly cheery set each night – it was exhausting to watch). The tour manager and the crew, alert to Steevi's temper, were spending long hours rigging and checking his gear, ensuring the show looked and sounded as immaculate as it could given its content, and Lana was going without soundchecks and playing to almost empty halls (Rex assured Marty that it would change once we were out of Texas, which was Steevi's home state, meaning that most of the tickets there had sold out before the support acts were added to the bill).

Allied to the torpid days of travel, life on the bus was a strange mix of tension and boredom that was affecting us all, the bad vibes hung over everything and there was a disconcerting feeling of barely contained violence, of something unwanted and shocking just around the corner that began to seep into everything that I was thinking. My sense of foreboding surrounded Iris too. As we got closer to Houston, I wondered what she would know after her few days with Brenna. I'd tried to reach her by phone several times but kept missing her (once speaking to a terse Brenna who gave nothing away; on another occasion, calling her office, I thought I'd heard her voice, a single word, 'no', whispered from the background) and during the long, silent sections of the journey there I became certain that Brenna had told her, and that she would either not be in Houston, or she would arrive righteously and rightfully angry and vengeful, or worse, betrayed, her fragile trust in the world further broken. The chaotic state of the tour seemed to demand further chaos, yet when we got there and I took a cab out to the airport to meet the flight that Marty had booked for her, I saw her walking through arrivals looking hard through the lines of people for us, and when she saw me her face cracked into a giant smile and she ran over, her heels clicking on the floor.

'Hey baby,' she said into my ear, and, as I felt it slip away, I realised exactly how much tension I'd been carrying.

'Hey,' I said, and wondered how much longer my luck would last.

*

On the cab ride back into town I told Iris about the tour so far.

'I don't know if I'm glad I missed it or not,' she said. 'You should be glad that you weren't in LA though.'

'Why's that?'

'Er . . . you know . . . *Donald* . . .'

'Oh, him.'

'Yeah, him. He came over to the office with this letter from Matthew that I have to give you. He calls like a hundred times a day.'

'A hundred.'

'Okay, four or five. But he keeps going on about the guy who runs the Temple of whatever . . .'

'Set.'

'Yeah. Says you must call him. Uggh. It sounds weird.'

'It's an occult organisation. They worship the Devil. It *is* weird, Iris.'

She gave her familiar little smirk. 'Well I'm glad it has nothing to do with me.'

'Yet.'

Iris punched my arm. It was good to have her back.

The cab took us through the skyscrapers of downtown.

Great blades of sunlight bounced from the buildings. These cities that they built here. The show was at a convention centre, amid vast, air-conned acres of giant halls and their many meeting rooms where people in suits with passes around their necks made endless crossings between them. It moved me for some reason. This was real life. They didn't seem unhappy. Marty took Iris away for a long meeting at which, Iris would tell me later, he could barely contain his panic and anger, so I went to join the band, who were 'resting' at the hotel. When I got there – a low-level HoJos on the other side of the freeway from the conference centre, the air-rush of the traffic still audible in the sagging reception area – I put Iris's bags on the bed and opened her case. On top of her clothes (mostly too small to fold – how I loved that girl), as she said it would be, was the letter from Matthew Trippe and, on a note attached to it with a paperclip (another very Iris moment) was Michael Aquino's telephone number. I lay back on the bed. We'd been on the bus for so long these last few days it felt as though I was still moving. I closed my eyes and wondered why Matthew had written to me. For a long time, ever since it had happened, in fact, Matthew's story had belonged to him, existed only for him and the few people that he had told. Even the people in Erie who had mocked him, and the organisation that surrounded Doc and Mötley Crüe that denied him were small and containable groups that would not warp his story and his idea of what it was. But once it came out in the magazine, and then, inevitably, in others, and the lawsuit went to court, then it would be examined in a new and different way and he might not be able to keep a grasp on it.

The envelope that held the letter was cheap and thin, and Matthew had pressed so hard when writing on it that the ink had bled into it, making my name look fuzzy, indistinct. Matthew's hand was an odd mix of cursive script with a couple of capital letters at random in the middle. I held it up to the light. There seemed to be some folded pages inside. I pulled Aquino's number off it and put it back in the case. As I did, I saw a diary tucked along one side. I didn't know that Iris kept one. I slid my hand inside it, prising the pages apart far enough to see that they were covered by Iris's hand, as tight and neat as Matthew's was weird and uncontrolled. I heard the sweat creak in my ears, crunched the lock on the door and did a second unconscionable thing.

*

Later, before Iris arrived back to shower and change for the gig, I called Michael Aquino. I guess I wanted some sort of reassurance that, whatever happened with the court case and the magazine piece and with Doc, that the story had some sort of life, some sort of truth. He spoke in the kind of clipped, no-bullshit sentences that came from two decades in the US Army. He said that he had undertaken many covert duties for them, psy-ops, attacking the enemy on a psychological plane, writing theory papers on mind wars, intelligence-gathering on a psychic level. He had led thought experiments with LSD and addressed methods of affecting the subconscious of his own soldiers and the enemy's. He had stressed the need for complete ethical integrity in the use of his ideas. He was, he said, still in receipt of the highest levels of security clearance. The army were aware that he was the high priest of the Temple of Set, and didn't discriminate against him any more or less than they would a Christian or a Mormon or a Scientologist. The Setian philosophy was one of individualism, freeing the self to act on its desires but also to aspire to a 'higher self' in shaping those desires. He considered his psy-ops work and his life as a high priest as parts of the same moral universe. I asked him about music. He said he liked the Doors and Jefferson Airplane. He told me about Matthew, how the Temple had taken him in, and how Matthew had displayed what Aquino called 'outstanding aptitude and intelligence'.

'He told me all about the Mötley Crüe,' Michael said. 'He was very convincing, but I have to tell you, I did not believe him.'

'No?'

'No, sir, I did not. His story kept changing. He had been involved in other criminality that I did not support or agree with. He had these boxes of what he called evidence, but it was circumstantial stuff. Nothing concrete.

'Now what I have to tell you next will sound strange to you. I travelled upon the upper planes. I looked at him there in the metaphysical way, do you understand that? I saw that he had truth in him and I decided to look for a sign of it. It took me some time, but I gained from the Library of Congress certain documents relating to the copyright of commercial properties – songs and so on – for Mötley Crüe and I can tell you that the social security number registered there for Nikki Sixx was the same number that was on Matthew's social security card that I was holding in my hand at the time. Those papers disappeared along with other pieces of his so-called evidence. I believe they were destroyed in a parole house or a rehab centre or something as a part of his so-called treatment but I saw them, and that is what I saw. That's what I wanted you to know.'

As soon as I replaced the receiver the phone rang, but when

I answered there was no one there, just the same empty, long-distance static that I had heard at the hacienda.

★

Hulme died in Tallahassee. By then the tour had wound through Louisiana and Alabama east into Florida, and much had happened. The phone calls went on, always when I was alone in a hotel room, which I often was as Iris and Marty were engaged in increasingly desperate efforts to make something happen for Lana. Finished copies of her album arrived in Corpus Christi on the same day that the magazine published the Matthew Trippe story (the name of the town a harbinger in my mind, which was now reading significance into anything and everything), and Iris and Marty spent long afternoons going from record store to record store offering stock, asking for signing sessions or window displays, sometimes dragging Lana with them. Iris worked every contact she had at radio and in local press, her efforts producing so little it was almost humiliating: nothing would have been better somehow. Each night Lana and the band went on in almost empty halls, the places only filling for the Germans and then Steevi, whose own sets were deadened by the complete breakdown of his relationship with Hulme, who was now permanently and overwhelmingly drunk, a looming, brooding presence who was becoming increasingly difficult to control. Even Rex had lost his cool, and he and Marty had engaged in a vicious slanging match in Baton Rouge in which accusations were countered by barely veiled threats, an argument that made for a poisonous few days until Rex softened and actually had Lana go on air with Steevi during a couple of his radio appearances – as close to an admission that the tour was a blowout as Marty was likely to get.

All of this had divided people into cliques. The Germans, long-time admirers of Nina, were now acolytes of Ray too – a couple had an interest in photography, or at least they did when Nina began allowing them to come along to the sessions that Ray was shooting with her. Tony and Doug were withdrawn, convinced they would be sacked at the end of the tour. Sylvio and I spent a few afternoons together in anonymous bars, but often I exiled myself to the hotel room with the excuse that I had the story about Lana to write. I began to anticipate the telephone calls. Sometimes I would listen in silence until whoever it was rang off, hoping for some kind of clue – a voice in the background, a placeable noise – but none came. Other times I shouted unexpectedly into the receiver, hoping to shock whoever was there, and one call I hung up on right away, and then I lifted the receiver thirty minutes later to find the heavy quiet of a long-distance connection still made. Only when I'd really cut loose with the shouting, ramming the receiver right to my mouth while I screamed some deranged abuse, did I seem to get something, a slight laugh, girlish and high.

When we'd crossed the Louisiana bayous, the bus had driven out over vast spans of water on arcing bridges, the grey ocean on one side of us and on the other an inland sea of rivers and inlets that cut between swamp palms and high water grasses, mile after mile of unguarded pathways. Anything could happen there. It was easy to imagine boats of unknown cargo and distant flags slipping through them unseen, with men like Doc awaiting news of their arrival.

I had with me a faxed copy of the Matthew story. As we travelled this brooding landscape I read it over – the magazine had done a nice job; the evidence compellingly presented – and I began to understand what it was really about, what it really meant. It was a story about transformation, the urge to become something different, to live in a world which you yearned for deeply but could not actually reach. The character of Nikki Sixx, if what Matthew said was true, had been inhabited by two people, their lives overlapping in a Venn diagram. The lives in each of the outer circles were chaotic and dark. Those circles were places of broken families, of nihilistic destruction, drugs and despair, and the odds against escape were almost incalculably high. To begin to do so first required the imagination to visualise it happening, to close the distance between what was real now and what might become real. Matthew John Trippe imagined so hard that he left himself behind and once he had done that he could never go back again. Nikki Sixx was not so much a person as a place created by two circumferences overlapping, a space that could be occupied by whoever could reach it. When the audiences looked up at the stage or listened to the records, they did not know Frankie Feranna or Matthew Trippe, they knew only Nikki.

How did it feel to yearn so hard to be someone else? How real did it have to appear before you believed it to be true? This was the real mystery.

'Who is Nikki Sixx?' the story on the fax paper in my lap began. Perhaps the person who really knew was not Frankie or Matthew but Doc; if Doc had done what Matthew said he had done, then he knew that Nikki Sixx was whoever happened to be on the stage wearing his tattoos and his make-up and playing his songs. Whoever the audience looked up and saw, that was Nikki, the man that Frankie and Matthew and many thousands of others dreamed that they might one day become.

★

What happened to Hulme was both shocking and inevitable, horrifying and yet deeply banal. I was twenty-three years old and unacquainted with the realities of death. I discovered for the first time how it comes from nothing.

Florida was supposed to be our nirvana. The tour catch-phrase had become 'It'll be alright once we get to Florida', a phrase that Rex had begun uttering while we were deep in the Southern badlands where the houses were half-sold and giant clouds hung dense and low in the oppressive heat. Florida promised clear skies and big crowds, college towns and name promoters, Rex's kind of place. His sense of equilibrium seemed to be returning at the thought of it. At the end of a show in Mobile, Alabama, the last before we crossed the state line into Florida and before a long-awaited two-day break in the schedule, he called everyone together in the production office and announced that the first three gigs in Florida were already sold out, and that he was adding an extra night in Miami. In addition, Steevi's album had just shipped gold. The Germans cheered. 'Fuck,' Hulme shouted from the back. 'Let's stay drunk . . .' Afterwards, Rex had slapped Marty on the back. 'Told you you'd get your money's worth . . .' and Marty had smiled for the first time in what seemed like days.

Iris and I rented a car and drove to Tallahassee alone. I'd been spending so much time in hotel rooms that I had a pocketful of unused per diems. Iris picked out a silver convertible and I uncreased the notes on the rental counter. We left Mobile at noon, when the sun was burning through the clouds, and for the first hour or so of the drive neither of us said very much. It was liberating enough to be away from other people. The road was almost empty, a long, two-lane highway lined by towering trees and with a wide meridian of grass between the carriageways in which carrion crows flew to shelter whenever we drove past the carcasses of animals that had been killed on the road. The crows seemed to wait until the last possible moment before leaving their meal, unfurling big black wings and half flying, half hopping to the grass divide. 'Ugh,' said Iris, the first time she saw some. I remembered something from school about them being auguries, unlucky omens because they used to flock near battle-fields and wait until they could feast on the dead. I held off telling Iris that one. Occasionally the road would narrow and we would pass through small and dusty towns that looked more like movie sets than real places, with their battered wooden churches and abandoned motels.

Iris studied the free map that she found in the glovebox and found a short detour that took us on to a glorious, hidden section of coast, where we stopped for gas and ate burgers at a beach shack. It was there, as I finally relaxed a little, that I realised how tense I had become. Iris must have felt it too. She sat down with her back to the sea and her face seemed to have a little more colour. She pulled out a couple of her dead-eye imitations – Marty's fraught voice as he asked bored record store assistants if they'd rack Lana's album by the door; then Lana urging an almost empty hall to shout Sylvio's name. I reached out and held her face in my hands for a moment. The sun had warmed one side and not the other.

'This is better, isn't it?' I said.

'Hmm, yes it is.'

I told her about the telephone calls that had been coming to the hotel rooms and how they made me feel. I told her that I thought they had something to do with the story of Matthew John Trippe. I didn't mention – because it hadn't

occurred to me until the moment that I had begun to talk –
that they had actually started at the hacienda.

'It's probably that dick Donald,' Iris replied. 'Or maybe
it's a female admirer of yours, calling to make sure I'm not
there . . .' She smirked.

'Okay, okay . . . I'm a dick, I know. It's just . . .' My sentence
tailed off.

'Forget it,' she said. 'This place is full of cranks. Now I have
something to tell you. You know that Marty was thinking of
hiring a private detective to find out if Lana was seeing
someone?'

I didn't, but I nodded anyway.

'Well, he asked me if I thought it might be you . . .'

'Thank God,' I said. 'There's someone more paranoid than
me on this tour. What did you tell him?'

'By the time I'd stopped laughing I didn't have to . . .'

'Very good,' I said. I took her hands across the table.

'What I actually said was that it's strange how some guys
can't see it – that a girl's in love with them.'

'Maybe. He's hung up because she's beautiful and hot and
he's . . .'

'He's not so bad,' Iris said. 'He looks a little like Michael
Douglas.'

'Ha! A very little . . . they're both humans I suppose . . .'

'Idiot . . .'

She rapped my shin with her foot but then kept it there. It
felt good. We finished the food and I pulled her over on to
my lap so we could both look out over the secret bay. The
wind blew in warm zephyrs, the light softening as the sun
dropped behind shimmering clouds and then as they passed
and exposed it again it cast giant rays downwards to the water,
blades so solid it seemed like it might be possible to touch

them. Gentle waves broke on the rocks. It was magnificent. Neither of us said anything but we held one another tight. Finally we walked back to the car and drove to the highway that took us into Tallahassee just as darkness fell. It was the last time we would truly be alone.

They discovered Hulme the next afternoon in his hotel room. He had missed some band meeting or other and Rex went to find him. When he got no answer, he knew the drill: the duty manager had a pass key and they went in together. Rex already had his hand on the hundred-dollar bills in his pocket, ready to hand a couple over when they found Hulme passed out on the bed in a drying pool of urine or unconscious next to some rail-thin bleach-blonde chick with bite marks on her neck, but instead they found the bed untouched and the bathroom door open, and when they looked inside, Hulme's huge frame, stiff and greying, the eyes and mouth open, confronted them, his death obvious in the great stillness that only the dead can have. In the slow horror of the moment, Rex would recall later the revulsion at himself as he realised that his first emotion had been relief.

In the days that followed rumour attached itself to Hulme, as if death itself weren't enough. The following was said and heard by people who were not there and did not know: that the body was surrounded by drug paraphernalia – used needles, torched foil, burned-up lighters. That he had been found in the bath with his wrists opened by deep vertical cuts, the bath overflowing with water turned purple by the blood, his corpse almost drained. That the body showed signs of a systematic beating given by the family of an underage girl who had slipped crying from the room at some point during the night. All of them were so ludicrously wide of the banality of what had actually happened. There were no needles or bathfuls of blood, no baseball bat with splinters of bone embedded in its tip, no suicide, no vampires or howling coyotes or conspiracies or mystery, just a lost man who had drunk himself into a coma so deep that his system found it impossible to restart. Iris and I arrived in time to stand with other members of the touring party, all of us ashen and shaken, behind the police tape that had been hastily erected around what they told us was now a 'crime scene', and see the gurney wheeled out by four paramedics who struggled to move it smoothly, Hulme's sheeted form hanging over each end. For some reason the sound of those wheels scraping over the concrete was the thing that really stayed with me, that and the absolute silence in which we watched it happen.

Remarkably, the show that night went ahead. Word had spread from local TV news to MTV, and the story led their bulletins, and soon the car park at the venue was filled with hastily made cards, flowers, soft toys, the atmosphere respectful and subdued (Ray and I walked around while he took some photographs, explaining gently to a couple of angry faces who queried him that he had a job to do) and for the first time, Lana went on to a full house, the band responding with the best set I'd seen them play. One of the Germans stepped in on lead guitar for Steevi's show (all of the reviews and stories, including mine, noting that he had been such a fan of Hulme's that he knew all of his parts; I found out long before the piece actually ran that Rex had been rehearsing him for a week, fearing that Hulme's relationship with Steevi would dissolve to the point where he would have to act).

It was an emotional night, for once the gesture of the crowd holding lighters in the air seemed genuinely touching, and it was evident that Steevi was still in shock, his mumbled intros sometimes tailing off, drowned by supportive cheers from the floor. There was a brief discussion of continuing to Orlando and Miami for the remaining shows, but Steevi's state of mind and Rex's discovery that his insurances were rock solid led to a swift and necessary cancellation, Marty remaining subdued even when Rex told him that the payouts would mean the refund of some of his buy-on.

With everyone anxious to get back to LA there was a scramble for flights and Ray and I volunteered to stay on an extra day. Iris took the final seat and I drove her to the airport at Tampa in the convertible, but the night had its chill and the wind on the freeway was up so Iris closed the roof as we rushed to make her plane.

*

Ray and I flew the following evening, both of us drained, Ray stoic after a couple of beers and happy to sit in silence but for the pitch of the engines. I wondered what we were flying back to. The Hyatt or the Sunset Marquis or the Mondrian, the Roxy, the Rainbow, the Tropicana, the Strip with its endless bands and its endless features to be written, all of them different, all of them the same. Ray had been doing it ten years longer than me. There were guys at the magazine ten years older than Ray. The plane flew higher into the black. Through the window I saw lights in the reaches beyond us, other planes, other craft, other stars. Stories told by the US military pilot I'd once sat next to, the pull of space, the mysteries of light. Things out there that no one understood. I drifted in and out of sleep in the way that only happens on aircraft at night. There had been one more call to the hotel room after I'd left Iris. It was silent again, but then I heard something that I thought I recognised – the screech of birds that I had heard once before, on the night that Iris and I had stayed in the chalet at her father's house. I'd tried to convince myself that I was wrong. As we parted in Tallahassee I said I'd meet her back at the house on Fountain Avenue, but a part of me, hard and unyielding, knew that she would not be there.

★

Ray and I got to the Hyatt late and didn't bother with the bar. I awoke the next afternoon and went through various faxes from Geoff (the Matthew Trippe story was being syndicated everywhere; Doc had sent a letter that was running in the next issue denying it all, accompanied by plenty of evidence that undermined Matthew's version of events; amongst the industry and the readers opinion was divided as to the story's truth) and from Donald, who was feeling the weight of Doc McGhee's legal presence.

Later, I took a cab out to Fountain. The house looked empty, and there was no reply when I knocked on the door. I sat on the step and waited. After a while I heard movement, and the latch slid back. It was Brenna.

'I didn't hear you, I was over at the pool.' She looked at me blankly. 'She's gone,' Brenna said after a moment. 'To her father's place for now. You know why.'

'For fuck's sake Brenna . . .'

'Exactly,' she said and closed the door.

I walked back to Sunset and found a cab. At the Hyatt, Ray was arranging a flight back home. The story on Lana was done, and there was nothing keeping us here now. We'd be back soon enough. I called the agent and booked mine too.

We had a night to kill. Ray went to the bar. I couldn't face it. I lay on the bed and watched *Headbanger's Ball*. Ratt, Poison, Faster Pussycat, White Lion, Vain, BulletBoys, Black Crowes,

Enuff's Z'Nuff, Guns N' Roses, Great White, Mötley Crüe. After a while I got my bag and packed my things. In a rucksack pocket was Matthew's letter, still unopened. After Tallahassee, I'd kind of forgotten about it. I showered and found a cleanish pair of jeans to put on. From the front pocket I pulled $150 in lost per diems and from the back the business card that the sexy vampire waitress had given me at Marty's party what felt like an age ago.

I laughed at the gods and reached for the phone.

★

Letter from Matthew John Trippe, read in transit,
LA–London, October 1988

Hey,

Hope that Donald gets this to you. I don't think I know who I am any more. There was a person once called Matthew but people hated him and they still do. All ~~these~~ the people in Erie, Pennsylvania. That's okay – I hated him too. He was a dick (!!!), and I didn't want to be him any more. So fuck him and goodbye dude!!!

I know that I met Mick Mars (Bobby Deal) in the Troubadour Lounge in 1983 like I said. That's what matters. Bobby knows it too, ~~though he won't say it now.~~ I was Nikki Sixx for a while there and then the other Nikki came back!! So who was I when he did?? That's what I think about ~~all the time~~.

My girlfriend has our kid and I have no money. I know what Donald says but I'm not dumb!!! Even if I won this case I wouldn't see the money, because it just goes on for years and Doc would never pay. Some days I think about what I'll do with it ($$$$) if I get it, but I know that's not real. BUT I AM REAL!!! HA HA!!

So dude, what would you do? COME ON HA HA!!! Could you tell people who you really are if you didn't know? I've said a lot of lies man, but FUCK dude, some of those lies are true!!! They are still playing my songs on the radio, and that feels good.

Okay dude, thanks for listening to my shit!!! Wish me luck bud!!!

Your friend,

Matt

NEWS
2008

From a distance, I watched the music industry crumble and fall into the sea with all the suddenness of a CGI disaster movie, its once-gleaming structures brought down by technology and the apparently limitless apathy of a generation of kids with a thousand other things to do. The lifestyle that we had enjoyed disappeared with it and in its place came something far smaller and more pragmatic. Bands that had seemed indestructibly big and famous had just one market left: nostalgia, and all of the sadness that it held. Their names and faces began to fade and for a long time I never thought about them at all.

I'd stayed at the magazine for another three years, and even then the scene on the Sunset Strip was diminished by the moral austerity of a new decade, its hedonism and party-hardy world view suddenly deeply unfashionable and in its place a fragile and nihilistic era that had pretensions to be far more 'meaningful' but instead just seemed dreary and unappealing. On the occasions that I returned to LA it seemed a more edgy and desperate place to be, and perhaps my appetite for it all was fading. Iris had gone of course and once, when a cab took Fountain to cut out the evening traffic on Sunset, I'd passed the house there but the lights were off and it looked empty and dark.

The gaps between trips got longer, the chance of a desk job on another magazine came along and then another and once that had come to an end I knew I had to get out of

writing about music altogether or become one of the guys I'd
seen grow old there, lifers who were so absorbed by it that
the years had gone by without them realising or taking their
chance of escape. I had gone, and once I was out it began to
seem like a small and distant place that I would never return
to. I moved away from England, wrote other stories, did other
things. The years passed. The industries I worked in – news-
papers, magazines, publishing – had a reckoning of their own,
but as they wrangled with that, the Internet cast new light on
a past that grew bigger every day, and once it had arrived no
one could disappear any more. On quiet days I would sometimes journey there, names and faces returning to a screen,
their stories taking unexpected turns, no longer safe and calm
where I had left them.

Ray and I stayed in touch for a while, a friendship I picked
up and put down too casually and it wasn't until some months
after it happened that I discovered he had died quite
suddenly, my shock and sadness nothing compared to that
of those close to him, but still enough to drag me back into
some days of reconnection. I couldn't think of Ray without
thinking of Lana, and she too had withdrawn into a different
life. She must have persuaded Marty that the failure of her
record meant something, because she didn't make another
and anyone searching her name online would find her
arrested in time, the results petering out decades ago. I knew
enough about her to look further, and one afternoon I discovered her and Marty on a property registry in LA, living in a
glorious house up in the hills, the owners of several busi-
nesses and Marty at the head of a law practice too. At the
request of an editor I sent an email asking if she'd like to
do a 'where are they now?' story and received a polite but
firm 'no' in reply. Blair had produced several movies and had

married and then quickly divorced a semi-famous actor – she shimmered glossily from images of premieres and awards ceremonies.

Sylvio was in LA too. On one of his websites (there were several, all dedicated to different albums and projects that sounded grandiose and successful) I found a review, attributed to me and appearing in 'the London *Times*' (a newspaper I had never written for) that called him 'world famous' and 'one of the greatest guitarists ever', sentences that I had never uttered but that made me smile because I could imagine Sylvio laughing as he made them up. I didn't mind, but there were other names on his sites that would, writers who had regarded him as a joke but who were now apparently proclaiming his brilliance. The sites were full of other claims too: awards he had received (an 'LA Music Award' for 'Humanitarian of the Year' and – of course – 'Guitarist of the Year'); a paragraph from 'the Dali Museum' eulogising a 'magical' song he had written inspired by the artist; lines from local hospitals and charities thanking him for donations. There were pictures of him with his arms around celebrities, stories of his gigs and sessions with famous musicians. The stories there were like the ones of his gig with Carlos Santana, slowly but significantly told and retold until their meaning changed and got greater. It was slightly unsettling, partly because it was so easy to see through and partly because I wondered how he could sustain it. But this was the Internet, and who was not reshaping their reality on there?

As for Iris, I yielded sometimes to the urge to see her out there in the high reaches of cyberspace, and I found enough to know that she too was out of music, but her virtual presence was fleeting and transient, the detail of her life hazy and unavailable. One drunken night I had sent an email and immediately regretted it (that hadn't stopped me checking constantly for a reply that never came, and I eventually convinced myself that perhaps my message had gone to a dead address).

For no good reason, my luck began to change. I had word from England that a book I'd written was to be reprinted: new jacket, quotes from reviewers, the works. A few people from this other life called and asked me to write stories for their big magazines. I got offered a job writing features for a city newspaper. Some weeks later, my copies arrived. They looked good, but still felt somehow fraudulent, not real. I wondered if other writers felt that way, but I didn't know any to ask and I didn't really want to. The publisher asked if there was anyone I'd like to send one to, and on a whim I searched again for Iris, found an address and passed it along.

Months afterwards, when I'd once more convinced myself that the lead was another dead end, the publisher forwarded a letter and I recognised her hand right away.

*

I hadn't written about music for a long time. I was reading wire reports at the newspaper one morning when something came up about Kiss. After some fractious years when they'd been down to a core membership of two, Gene Simmons and Paul Stanley, they were back playing shows with their original guitarist Ace Frehley. Ace was a well-known fuck-up who would often be too out of it to play properly, but now he was also back on the straight and narrow. And then some fans at one of their shows had become suspicious when something about Ace didn't seem right. Because the band played in make-up it was hard to be sure, but they were pretty certain that the man they'd seen on stage wasn't him. They looked at some photos and spoke to other fans and started complaining and the band's management had to come out and admit that Ace had been unable to play at those shows, and rather than cancel them another guitarist had put on his costume and played the gigs. I found a quiet office, shut the door and for the first time in many years, typed the name of Matthew John Trippe. As I entered it into the search engine, I wondered why it had taken me so long to come back to him. The results flashed up, and I began to read.

The first parts of the story returned to me quickly. While Matt waited for his lawsuit to make its way through the courts, his growing notoriety had brought plenty of offers from bands and managers. He'd got some studio time and made some demos but he'd behaved like an asshole and fucked everything up. He walked out of sessions and smashed up a new guitar that a manager had bought for him. Soon he was back in Florida with his girlfriend and a young child and no money, he said, to buy diapers. Donald seemed to have faded from the scene. In December 1993, he dropped his lawsuit for the final time. By then, Doc was no longer manager of Mötley Crüe. The music business had changed quite radically. Mötley Crüe had sold millions of records and played several huge tours and they had all made many millions of dollars but their style of music had been swept away by another generation. Matthew did face Doc once in court, and Doc had called him 'a sick little puppy', which made me smile. Things began to go Mötley Crüe's way again when they published a tremendous tell-all book called *The Dirt*, which became a best-seller. It contained hundreds of wonderfully depraved and salacious anecdotes, but it didn't mention Matthew at all. Other speculation about Matthew was still out there. I found an interview with a guy who'd been in a band with him. He'd said: 'He looked a lot like Nikki Sixx. Maybe a little heavier but the facial features were very similar. A variety of photos seemed to show differences in facial features through those years for Nikki Sixx. That could be attributed to any number of things though, I guess. Matt was at the time that I knew him, a member of the Temple of Set, which is a pretty exclusive organisation. I find it a little strange that they would allow some weird-guy-nobody with no money to be a member, but I guess it could happen. He could at times be very convincing, and to this day, I don't know whether or not anything he said was true.'

I was pretty sure of one thing: that Matthew believed it was true. He had slipped into the centre of that Venn diagram and he had lived as Nikki Sixx, at least in a way and at least for a while. It seemed like a story to me. It was rooted in a very particular time and place, and could only have happened when it did, when those kinds of mysteries could survive in the way that the disguising of Ace Frehley could not. I was due in Las Vegas to write about a boxing match, and within a couple of days I had altered my ticket and I was flying into LA.

*

The cab ride on the 405 was strangely evocative, the traffic on the freeway, the towering palms, the giant billboards coalescing into something timeless and familiar. Iris's email had arrived hours before I flew. It was short and slightly opaque (mine had been overlong, eager to explain why I was in LA), but she wanted to meet and suggested a place. My head was still buzzing with the phantom noise of the plane engines when I checked into the hotel – some boutique place in West Hollywood – and got online. There were two videos I wanted to watch. One was of a rambling, three-hour interview Matthew had given to a local radio station, and the other was of Sylvio.

At first I barely recognised Matthew. He looked very different now, his hair short and badly cut, his face puffy, any resemblance to Frank Feranna or the avatar of Nikki Sixx destroyed by the hardships of his life. Many of those appeared self-inflicted. He still had the strange sing-song way of overcoming his stammer, and he still made long digressions when asked simple questions, the rise and fall of his voice matching the rise and fall of his story, which he seemed to have embellished further in parts. I knew now that his life would always have this mystery at its centre. It was the one story he had to tell.

After a while I grew tired of watching him. I took a break. The hotel had a courtyard garden warmed by heat lamps that sent an amber glow up into the palms, silhouetting them against the hills beyond. The night wind was chilling, despite the lamps. The LA feeling was back – the haunted hills, the great silence out there. It was still exact, just at I remembered it.

I went back inside to watch Sylvio. A deeper connection was suggesting itself as I did. This was another interview, another radio station, this one in Las Vegas. The DJ, a harassed thirty-something with a hip haircut, seemed unprepared. Sylvio sat next to him. Aside from having dyed his hair blond, he looked the same: tanned, his white shirt open to the waist, chains and charms around his neck. The DJ read from his script. He introduced Sylvio as 'a world famous' musician, producer and philanthropist who was in the studio to promote a CD of 'unreleased material' by Jimi Hendrix that he'd produced. Sylvio took a pull on a long cigar he was smoking and began to talk. It was transfixing. He'd obviously entered another place as he closed his eyes and talked about his friendships with Keith Richards and Johnny Depp. He told the story about jamming with Carlos Santana ('he always likes to drag out his friends to play with him'). He said that he and Keith Richards had 'worked together' on an album called *The Precious Stones*. He announced that he and Keith were going to work on a new record together. The DJ looked at him, astonished.

'So you're producing the next Stones album?' he asked.

'Yeah,' said Sylvio after a moment, 'I am.'

He said that he'd put Keith Richards together with Scotty Moore for one of the songs. He started talking about how Keith had appeared with Johnny Depp in a film and how Johnny, who happened to be a friend of his too, wanted to be on the album and Sylvio had magnanimously agreed. Then Johnny had suggested that Iggy Pop be on the album, 'so we're going to have a lot of special guests'.

The DJ asked him what he would do after that and he said he wanted to work with Jimmy Page 'and get the best out of him', because other producers were 'shit scared' to ever tell someone like Jimmy that he could play better. The DJ stared at him, unsure what to ask next. I realised why: he was wondering how he'd never heard of someone as 'world famous' as Sylvio, with all of these friends and all of these connections. He just looked at him for another long second and then shook his hand.

'Well I wish you luck with it.'

'Thanks,' said Sylvio. 'I'm going to need it,' and he laughed.

★

There were several other clips of him online, mostly just terrible videos he'd made of him performing various cover versions (I'd watched them all many times. He was usually surrounded by women in their underwear, smoking a cigar and drinking champagne while they kissed him and rubbed his chest), but I understood that the interview was where he had crossed the line, where he'd stepped into the same space in the diagram that Matthew had. It had been happening in his head since I first knew him, but now he had externalised it, brought it into the world. He couldn't stop it once he had.

I got some sleep, the deep but unsatisfying kind that only travelling through time zones can offer, and the following day walked down the Strip to get the final part of the Sylvio story. In a Denny's between the Hyatt (which I noticed as I passed had been renamed – something bijou and boutique) and the building that used to be Tower Records (my ghosts of Sunset now, to go with all of the other ghosts of LA) I met with a former record company executive who specialised in tracking down and restoring jazz and country recordings from the beginning of the twentieth century. He'd won several Grammys for the box sets that he had made from them. He'd been introduced to Sylvio through mutual friends, and Sylvio had told him about his plans to bring that kind of music into the modern age. They set up a talent competition to find a new 'jazz idol' (it was quickly shut down on copyright grounds and the entry fees apparently never returned) and they planned a new box set of recently discovered bluegrass recordings. The set was announced in the press with the executive's name attached and a German conglomerate provided $500,000 to begin production. Then the money disappeared and Sylvio had become vague and defensive and finally stopped coming to meetings or answering calls.

The executive spent the next year trying to repay people who had pre-ordered the set and to repair the damage to his reputation. A lawyer advised him that Sylvio might have done something similar in the past, so he began searching for his name online and making his way through the maze of websites that promoted Sylvio's various projects and charities.

He ordered more coffee and a while later we were joined by two of the men that he had found. Each had met Sylvio in LA and had been taken in by his stories of Keith Richards and Jimi Hendrix and Carlos Santana. They had visited his large house in a gated community and sat by the pool as they parted with substantial sums of money in return for percentage points in the albums that Sylvio was about to put out, albums that featured the great and the good of rock 'n' roll. In return for $30,000, one had received a cheque for $52.17. The other had invested $15,000 and had been astonished to receive the finished CD, which came in an ill-fitting case and contained a barely audible interview with Hendrix that lasted for just a few minutes before giving way to Sylvio's cover versions of Jimi's songs.

Together they had gone to the public prosecutor's office and he had begun an investigation that brought forward more people with similar stories: childhood friends, music business wannabes, aspiring musicians, people who had met Sylvio in bars and restaurants and at parties at his house and listened to his plots and his plans. He was charged with multiple counts of securities fraud relating to running a Ponzi scheme, and, after a brief chase by police once he realised he was about to be arrested (he'd locked up the house and got in his car to drive to the state line), he had engaged a lawyer and entered a plea bargain with the prosecutor in which he accepted one charge and had fourteen others on the file, and in return he was sentenced to three to eight years in prison, ordered to pay restitution of hundreds of thousands of dollars and told that he was subject to deportation from the United States upon his release. The single charge that he accepted pertained to an album of cover songs 'featuring artists such as Carlos Santana and Prince' for which he had taken an investment of more than $39,000 from a single individual, of which $820.22 had been used to manufacture the record and the rest retained for Sylvio's 'unauthorised use'. In return he had issued a single royalty payment of $63.60.

Afterwards I walked back to the hotel and took my laptop into the shaded courtyard. I found another of Sylvio's films. This one was a little older, some footage of an album launch party at his house. It began with the camera panning around a large room, expensively decorated with a faux hippy shabby-chic vibe: deep leather sofas, scatter cushions, decorative rugs hung on the walls. Happy-looking people – none of whom I recognised – milled around drinking beer and laughing. The camera lingered for a moment on a column in the open-plan living area; on it were framed pictures of (a much younger) Sylvio with Carlos Santana and other B-league rockers, and a gold record that I recognised immediately as the one he'd got when Lana's song had appeared on the compilation album all that time ago. The camera swept across the room again and settled on Sylvio, seated on one of the huge sofas next to a fawning interviewer waving a microphone at him. He was smoking a cigar and playing with a book of matches as he spoke. I could tell he'd had a couple of beers by the way he cracked his bad jokes and then looked straight down the camera. In those moments I could see the man he once was, a fleeting glance at his younger, lighter self, almost gone now, obscured by the power of this fantasy existence, and then he realised he had an album to sell, and he began to tell the world once again about his amazing, astonishing life.

★

That afternoon, after I'd called Doc McGhee's office and been told that he wasn't available or even in the country, I slept in a half-fugue state, odd and unsettling dreams constantly re-directed by external noise – a television blaring from an adjoining room, the traffic beginning to build up on Sunset – and people and images appearing in odd combinations. Sylvio arrived in the Denny's to tell me that he was out of prison now and he wanted us to drive up to Marty's house in the hills to make an album with Lana. He said Ray should come too, and I had to tell him that Ray was dead. In the dream that came closest to the surface, Iris kept calling to reschedule our meeting, and every time I set out to go, she would call again to change the venue.

'Don't worry my dear,' she would say, 'we'll do it tomorrow . . . We'll do it tomorrow . . .'

★

I hired a car and drove out to meet her. Iris had texted some directions. They took me through Pacific Palisades, which had the same suggestions of absence behind the towering fences that I recalled from decades before, the memories powerful now, almost overwhelming, and I was glad to reach the Pacific Coast Highway and float along the coast to the place that Iris had picked out, a beachside restaurant, obviously expensive, with tables on a deck that looked out over the ocean. I saw her right away, sitting with her back to the entrance, her hair still long, her posture offering a heavy jolt of recognition. I waited for a moment. Now that I was here, I wasn't sure I wanted to be. For an instant I thought of walking away, but then I'd already done that. She turned around.

'Well . . .' she said.

I could tell immediately that she was strong now, stronger than me. We looked at one another. The years suited her. She was still pale, but luminously beautiful. She leaned across the table and kissed me, briefly. Instant recognition really.

'You look the same,' she said.

'Thanks, I wish I did.'

She gave her little smirk. Had forgotten about that, but it was good to see it. I began to feel better. The waiter kept hovering. That was the problem with expensive places. I ordered something without looking at the menu. Didn't really care about the food, but it came anyway and went mostly uneaten. Iris toyed with hers too. The waiter came back several times to ask if everything was alright.

'Can you leave us alone for a while?' Iris said evenly. This was the new her, obviously. The waiter walked off huffily.

'You know', I said, 'apart from driving you to the airport, the last time we were together was on a beach too. The evening before Tallahassee.'

'Oh yes . . .' she said. 'You're right . . . And then Hulme . . .'

'He's been dead for so long now. I think about that – all of the years he's missed. It makes it seem so far away.'

'What has he missed? With you I mean. Are you married?'

I told her everything (perhaps I spoke for so long because I didn't want to hear her answer the same question) and then I went on, telling her about Matthew and then Lana and Marty and then the story of Sylvio.

Iris excused herself to visit the restroom and I saw her bag on the floor lying carelessly open, the inside full and messy, and it reminded me for some reason of her bedroom at the hacienda, her belongings strewn over the giant bed, suitcase flung open at one end. I felt a great wave of sorrow break over me, all of the sadness and regret that had been inside somewhere for so long rising up with an unexpected force. I watched her walk back to the table in her elegant clothes. She sat down and took my hand. 'I can't stay too much longer . . . Let's not leave it unsaid . . .'

She was right. Brave and right.

'I'm sorry Iris. You don't know how much . . .'

She held my gaze for a long time. 'Maybe I do,' she said.

It was Brenna who had told her father. He came to the house on Fountain and drove Iris out to the coast – they were there before my flight had even landed. Iris hadn't been particularly surprised by the news. When I'd taken her diary from her case while we'd been on tour and, with rising shame and self-disgust, read the last few pages before replacing it, I realised that the thought had already occurred to her ('I don't want to put down what might have happened in case it has,' she had written – words that I have found impossible to forget). Iris had her secrets too and she kept them well. I'd read a little more, enough to realise that Brenna's relationship with Iris's father had something to do with it all. They had been together and apart, Iris's father unwilling to take things further with her, she sleeping with other men and making sure that he found out, Iris caught somehow in the middle (I could only imagine how Brenna might have described what happened, and as every possibility was dreadful it was something I chose to drive from my mind).

Her father had died a couple of years ago. He had known it was going to happen, and had bought Brenna an apartment somewhere in Century City, but Iris had never visited and they saw one another rarely now. She still had the house on the coast and the hacienda.

'I shouldn't really say this but when he died, a part of me felt free . . .'

For a moment her eyes filled with tears, but she lifted her head and forced them back. I went to tell her about the phone calls, but stopped myself. The past loomed up for us both, too heavy now and too strong, connections made and then splintering, spinning up into space to the far reaches of zero gravity, where strange things flew. She looked at the almost empty beach, where a man and a little girl were walking hand in hand. She waved down to them. 'Ah, I have to go,' she said.

'Is that . . . ?'

'My step-daughter,' she smiled. 'She stays with us some-times. He's a good man. You'd like him . . .'

We stood up. She pulled me to her and I held her for the last time.

'I doubt that, Iris,' I said.

★

Letter from Iris M, received July 2007

Hello there,

So you did it – wrote a book. I knew that you would. Thank you for thinking of me and sending it. I liked it. Thank you for your note too. Yes, if you're ever in LA, look me up. It would be nice to meet. I'm still here, as you can see.

Too much has happened for this short reply, but I am happy, so you can relax silly boy . . .

You weren't the person that I thought, and that was my fault, not yours.

Love,

Iris